MASTER CLASSROOM MANAGEMENT
IN EIGHT WEEKS

MASTER CLASSROOM MANAGEMENT
IN EIGHT WEEKS

JERRY EVANSKI

Master Classroom Management in Eight Weeks

Copyright © 2015 by Jerry Evanski

Cover and book design by Jacob L. Grant

ISBN 978-1-9384064-7-8

Brigantine Media/Compass Publishing
211 North Avenue
St. Johnsbury, Vermont 05819
Phone: 802-751-8802
Fax: 802-751-8804
E-mail: neil@brigantinemedia.com

Dedication

To my wife, Mary,
and my two lovely daughters, Julia and Emily

Table of Contents

Introduction

This is a book about classroom management unlike any you have read before. Many teachers believe that the only component of classroom management is student discipline—managing student behavior through rules and consequences. Classroom management is much more than just coming up with rules and meting out consequences when those rules are broken.

Poor teaching strategies can trigger behavior problems. When a teacher gives confusing directions, could students respond with inappropriate behaviors? Absolutely. I see this happen all the time, even with experienced teachers. When students sit too long without a break will they create mischief? Without a doubt.

You can prevent problems before they occur. I have analyzed possible triggers for behavior problems in the classroom and have found ways for you to eliminate them proactively by using effective management strategies. Teachers who wait until students act out are constantly in a reactive mode with discipline issues.

Most new teachers learn how to create classroom rules to help manage their classrooms. New teachers also need to learn practical skills for implementing those rules, and so much more. They need to know how to get students' attention; how to engage students so they are sitting on the edge of their seats, waiting for the next part of the lesson; how to give students a needed break, yet maintain order in the classroom. You'll learn how to do this in the next eight weeks.

Classroom management styles can impact students for years in both positive and negative ways. In one study, first grade students who were rated by their teachers as being in the top quartile for aggressive behavior were randomly assigned to classrooms that were described as either well-run or chaotic. Years later in middle school, it was found that the students in the orderly, well-run classrooms in first grade had a 3 to 1 chance of still being highly aggressive in middle school. The students who were in the chaotic classrooms in first grade had an astounding 59 to 1 chance of being highly aggressive in middle school (Kellam et al., 1994).

The human brain wires itself differently as it interacts with the environment. This is the concept of neuroplasticity. The environment that students are growing up in today is vastly different than twenty or thirty years ago, and the brains of our students are wired differently. Take, for example, the huge amount of time today's students spend in isolation with an electronic device. The emphasis on fine motor skills, focusing on stationary objects such as a laptop or smartphone for hours at a time during critical developmental periods, watching videos that are only six seconds long—all these can affect students' ability to read off the board or sit for extended periods of time or have mental stamina for tasks that require sustained attention. The skills you will learn in this book will help you deal with your students' new brain wiring.

I often see teachers struggling to maintain order in the classroom, not knowing what to do in very complex and demanding situations. Many teachers spend an inordinate amount of time being drill sergeants, constantly disciplining students. This is not why we got into the profession of teaching.

Every teacher I know loves learning, loves students, and wants to share his or her love of learning with students. When the skills in this program are mastered, you will have the ability to manage your classroom with confidence. Then you can go back to doing what you signed up for in the first place—teaching students the subjects that you love.

There are eight fundamental tasks that teachers engage in many times every day:

Getting Attention   **Getting Participation**

Keeping Attention   **Giving Directions**

Engaging Students   **Communicating**

Teaching the Lesson   **Transitioning**

When you perform these tasks well, your classroom hums along and your students are productive learners. When you handle these tasks poorly, your class can get out of control.

In the next eight weeks, you'll learn skills in all of these eight fundamental tasks that will help you manage your classroom. Each week will focus on one task. There are five skills to master for each task. Here's how it works:

Every day, Monday through Friday, you will be introduced to a new skill. Each skill has a short description and an explanation why the skill works. The directions for implementing each skill are described in detail. I suggest that you read about the skill and practice it first before you implement the skill with the students.

Then try the new skill with your class. To be most effective, you must implement the skill in front of a real, live classroom full of students. You may master some of the skills after one try and seamlessly incorporate them into your teaching repertoire. Others will require more practice over several weeks to make the skill a habit. In eight weeks, you will learn the skills you need to manage your classroom.

After a few months of practicing these new skills, find someone who will give you honest feedback. Ask a family member, a colleague, or a friend to watch you teach, either live or by viewing a recording of you teaching a lesson. Ask this person to tell you honestly what he/she thinks of your classroom management. It will help if you give your colleague this book before he/she observes you.

You'll need this feedback, because you may not realize how much you have learned and how these skills have changed the way you teach. An observer will help you understand just how far you've progressed.

As you work through the skills over the next eight weeks, you will build confidence over time. Start by doing one new skill each day. Commit to using that skill the first five minutes of the class's first hour. That's it for that day! After a while, you'll use the skill all morning, and eventually all day.

In eight weeks, you will have forty effective classroom management skills at your command. Let's move toward the classroom that hums along, and away from the chaotic classroom where the teacher isn't in charge.

...Starting now!

Week 1: Getting Attention

The first step to learning is paying attention. You can't teach if you don't have your students' attention. When they are engaged and interested in what's going on in your class, everyone benefits. Whether it is to give directions, begin a discussion, or transition to a new topic, the first essential step to effective classroom management is getting your students' attention.

There are three main ways we get information into our brains: visually (through the eyes), auditorily (through the ears), and kinesthetically (through movement of the body). Our brains constantly receive millions of bits of information from all of these systems. If we consciously paid attention to each bit of information, we would do little else but try to make sense of the cacophony of input. Luckily for us, Mother Nature created a wonderful system called the reticular activating system, or RAS. To get students' attention, you have to get the students' RAS to bring your signal for attention to their conscious awareness.

HERE'S THE RESEARCH

The reticular activating system is located in the brain stem, and lets into the brain's conscious awareness what information is important (Kinomura et al., 1996).

There are many factors involved in getting attention in a classroom. Students' attention will wax or wane depending on factors such as how interesting the presentation is to each student, how interested the learner is in the subject, how novel the information or presentation is, how meaningful the information is perceived to be by the student, and so on.

But classroom management starts with attracting the attention of every student in the class. This week, you'll learn how to get everyone's eyes on *you*!

There are five components for getting attention in Week One:

MONDAY	Signals	THURSDAY	Location Anchors
TUESDAY	Patterns	FRIDAY	Novelty
WEDNESDAY	Music Anchors		

Signals

An effective teacher needs a variety of signals to get the attention of the class. Some teachers use an auditory cue to get attention, such as a bell or a chime. That works, but after a while, the students get habituated to the sound of the bell and tune it out instead of recognizing the signal that it is time to tune in to you. Some teachers use a purely visual signal to get students' attention, such as turning off the lights. That can work, too, but you're not always near the light switch when you're teaching.

> **HERE'S THE RESEARCH**
>
> There are hundreds of millions of brain cells that are used to process visual information, which account for about thirty percent of the brain's cortex. In comparison, only eight percent of the cortex is dedicated to touch, and three percent to processing auditory signals (Grady, 1993).

A cue given by the teacher that is both visual and kinesthetic is a very effective classroom signal for attention. A kinesthetic cue activates several areas of the brain, including the brain stem, the motor and sensory cortices at the top of the brain, and the nerves and muscles involved in the movement.

Today's skill is a signal that will attract your students' attention so they are ready to learn. Read the directions, practice the skill, and then try it today with your class.

Skill: Cross Clap

Start your week by using the Cross Clap, a powerful signal to get students' attention that appeals to both the visual and kinesthetic regions of the brain.

Here's how to do it:

1 Stand in front of the class with a big smile, quickly making eye contact with as many students as you can. Your face should convey the message, "This is going to be fun!"

2 Hold your hands out, one above your head, one straight out in front of you, with both palms facing inward.

3 Say to the class, "Every time my hands cross, you clap."

4 Switch your hands vertically in front of you, so that the hand above your head moves down, and your lower hand moves over your head.

5 The students should clap each time your hands cross each other in the middle.

6 After three or four repetitions, start moving your hands, but trick the students by quickly stopping your hands from crossing. The students will clap anyway, and since it is a break in the pattern, they will laugh.

7 Now that you have the students' attention, begin to give your directions.

Explain and practice the Cross Clap before you want to start using it in class, so students understand how it works. After they know it, you can start using it to get your students' attention.

When you want to try the Cross Clap for the first time to get the students' attention, raise your hands as described in step one. Then catch the attention of two or three students in different parts of the room and mouth the words, "Are you ready?" with a big smile.

Switch your hands three or four times. More and more students will join in as you're doing the Cross Clap. When the class is quiet and watching you, give them your next directions.

After your class responds well to the Cross Clap signal, try some of these other signals to add some variety in your classroom:

- **Rhythm Echoes**
  Clap out a rhythm, and have the students echo the same rhythm back to you.

- **Lap-Clap-Snap**
  This signal works well for getting the attention of a whole classroom full of students, or even a full auditorium.

  Do this rhythm: hit your lap with both of your open palms, then clap your hands, then snap your fingers. As you do the Lap-Clap-Snap, count down each pattern; "Three" (lap-clap-snap), "Two" (lap-clap-snap), "One" (lap-clap-snap). After the last lap-clap-snap, all of the students will be quiet.

  In the classroom, stand in front of the room and start the lap-clap-snap pattern. Catch the eye of one student and say, "Join me when you can." After a few patterns, all the students will have joined in. Then countdown your lap-clap-snaps: "Three—two—one," and the class will be quiet and ready to listen.

Sit and Shhh!

Use this skill when students are moving around the room, and you want them to transition to sitting on the floor in front of you.

Turn some music on fairly loud. Then start to turn the music down (a remote control for the audio player can make this easier). As you turn the music down, sit down slooooowly. Your students will watch you and match your movements as you slowly sit down and turn the volume down. Time sitting and turning the volume down so that the music is gone at the exact moment you are fully seated.

Press Pause

Ask the students to press "pause." Demonstrate this cue by reaching above your eye level and press the imaginary *pause* button on an imaginary DVD player. Tell students that the DVD player is on a high shelf in front of them, so they have to reach up to press "pause." When they have pressed "pause" the students are quiet and ready to listen.

Patterns

WEEK 1

Today you are going to add to your repertoire of signals for attention.
    We learn and store information in patterns. Use a signal that creates a pattern to trigger the students' automatic response. Call and Response is a pattern that gets the whole class involved and paying attention immediately.

HERE'S THE RESEARCH

In call and response, the call activates the students' brains and makes them pay attention, an essential first step in the learning process. The call activates the reticular activating system, which is located in the brain stem and is responsible for filtering what our brains pay attention to (Pribram, 1975). After the call, the students will respond. The response is a habituated response that students will perform because they want closure and to be a part of the group, and will conform to the norm of the group (Allen and Wilder, 1980).

Skill: **Call and Response**

Here's how to do it:

1 Say the first part (the call) of a familiar phrase to the students.

2 The students then give the response to the call. As the students give the response, they simultaneously turn their bodies so they are facing you.

3 As soon as they give you the response, you immediately begin to give your next directions.

The following are calls and responses that work well with students:

Teacher	Students
"Here's the story…"	"Of a man named Brady"(to the tune of *The Brady Bunch* television show theme song)
"Whop bop-a-lu mop"	"A whop bam boom" (to the tune of *Little Richard's Tutti Frutti*)
"Ba-da-da-da-da"	"I'm lovin' it" (McDonald's jingle)

Try at least one of these today, or create a new one and try it with your class. Use part of your school's alma mater if everyone knows it, or a phrase from a song that's currently popular.

You could use the same call and response all year long, or change it from time to time. You can even have a new call and response every week. Introduce a new two-part phrase and practice it with the students. For example, one week the call is that you say "hot" and the students respond "dog." The next week the call is "Finding" and students respond "Nemo."

It's fun to have the students give you a new phrase every week to use. When you develop new calls and responses with your students, they are sure to remember them.

Music Anchors

An anchor on a ship keeps it in place. An anchor in a classroom attaches a certain behavior to a certain stimulus.

Human beings have excellent contextual memories. Specific locations can trigger memories. You may remember at which table you sat when you last ate at a restaurant, or which swing you were on in the playground when you fell and scraped your knee as a child.

HERE'S THE RESEARCH

Music can also act as a powerful contextual cue to trigger memories (Smith, 1985).

Specific music can be used to anchor behaviors. For example, the "think" music from the game show "Jeopardy!" makes anyone who hears it stop for a second and think about answering a question—any question! Teachers can use music to help make some classroom activities into a routine, and if you use upbeat, fun music, you can even anchor a good feeling to the activity.

Music anchors can automate many classroom routines throughout the day. Not a word from you needs to be said. You just play the appropriate anchor music and the students respond accordingly.

The music anchor you will learn today is for making the morning routine easier, which I call, appropriately enough, morning music!

Skill: Morning Music

Here's how to do it:

1. You need a device to play music, such as an iPod or mp3 player, cell phone, computer, or CD player. Using a device that allows you to create a playlist can be helpful for easily finding the specific music you want.

2. Decide what your morning music anchor will be. The musical selection needs to be long enough to give students time to put away coats, get out textbooks, finish any last minute homework and turn homework in—whatever your

morning tasks are before class starts. I suggest an upbeat song set to relatively low volume. "Happy" by Pharell Williams works well for many age groups.

3 Today, begin by explaining to your students that you will be playing some music as they come into class, and then play them a few seconds of the song you have chosen.

4 Tell them that this is their morning music. During this song, the expectation is that they will complete all of the usual morning tasks, including putting away their materials, finishing up and turning in any homework, and other specific tasks you have in your classroom, like signing up for lunch or taking attendance.

5 Let students know that by the end of the song, they should have all tasks completed and be sitting at their desks, ready to learn.

6 Play the morning music and monitor your students as they perform their morning tasks. When the music is finished, check that everyone is seated and ready to start working. If the song is too long or too short, adjust it for the next week.

Add to your music anchors throughout this week:

- **Other routines**
  Throughout your school day, try using other songs to anchor routine activities, such as cleaning up, lining up, or giving time to begin homework assignments. You could use music to automate many of the repetitive routines that occur throughout the day.

- **Mood music**
  Select music with the right mood for each activity. For example, if you are having students clean up at the end of the day, music with a fast tempo is appropriate. If you are playing music while students are getting a start on their homework, a slower, instrumental piece fits the mood better.

- **Reminders**
  For the first few days, remind students of the expectations for each piece of music. After three or four reminders, when you start playing the music, the activity should automatically occur.

Location Anchors

Anchoring locations to specific activities is a technique that works extremely well. It primes students' brains for the activity that happens in that spot.

Most teachers have a teaching spot at the front of the room. This spot is where you naturally stand to teach or write on the board. It is usually in the front of the room. Often it's not just a single spot—it's an area in which you walk, lecture, and conduct discussions while teaching.

Recognize exactly where *your* teaching spot is, and anchor that location firmly in your students' minds by always teaching from that place, and *only* teaching from that place. That area of the room should only be used for the purpose of teaching.

You might find other location anchors for activities, such as telling a story in the story spot or showing dissatisfaction in the bad news spot. If you are meticulous about this and only do certain activities in specific locations, that activity will be anchored in the minds of the students and you'll get their immediate attention when you move to that place in the room.

HERE'S THE RESEARCH

Our visual systems have a high capacity for learning and retaining repeated spatial context (Jiang, Song, and Rigas, 2005). Research is clear that having an anchored visual context, such as a story spot, will guide spatial attention toward the location, and the students will begin to anticipate that you will tell a story when you stroll over and stand in that location (Chun and Jiang, 1998).

Skill: Your Teaching Spot

Here's how to do it:

1 Recognize where *your* teaching spot is and its natural boundaries.

2 Before the day begins, mark the boundaries of your teaching spot with tape if that helps you remember to always teach from that area. Be sure to teach from your teaching spot all day. As the day goes along, your students will begin to recognize the cue that when you move into your teaching spot, the lesson is about to start, and they will pay attention.

3 Step out of the teaching spot when you aren't actually teaching a lesson. For example, you can move to another location when it's time for the class to get ready to move out of the classroom, or when the class has seatwork or group work, or when someone else has the attention of the class (such as another student, the principal, or a guest speaker).

Here is another important location anchor to incorporate into your classroom when the time is right:

• The Bad News Spot

If there is bad news to give, make sure to deliver it somewhere other than your usual teaching spot. But if you are in your teaching spot and the students won't quiet down, you may get angry and (maybe) even start to yell. After the class is quiet, you start teaching from the same place you just yelled from. Now you have confused your students. Avoid contaminating your teaching spot with bad news or negative feelings.

To deliver bad news, go to a corner of the room you don't often visit. You can also use this corner to communicate the classroom rules and consequences. Act stern to make sure that spot is anchored as the Bad News Spot. When the students know this is the anchor spot for communication when times are tough, you need to simply start walking toward that corner for the class to quiet down.

When you are finished giving the class the bad news, the slow walk back to the teaching spot not only gives some time to decontaminate the negative energy in the room, but also allows you to regain composure, catch your breath, and refocus on the lesson at hand.

I have a friend who is a brilliant teacher. He has an ugly necktie that hangs in his Bad News Spot, in an area of the classroom to which he rarely goes. He has described very seriously to the students that the tie represents his dissatisfaction with their behavior, and it represents his anger and disappointment with them. All he has to do is point in the direction of the tie hanging there and say "Do I have to put on . . . the tie?" Just the reminder is usually enough for the students to get it together.

Novelty

As teachers, we have to find a good balance between novelty and routine. Too much routine and not enough novelty can create boredom. (But watch out—too much novelty and not enough routine can cause chaos.)

HERE'S THE RESEARCH

Novelty and surprise can stimulate students' attention and can promote a state of eager motivation (Hunkin et al., 2002).

A novel stimulus in the environment can trigger the orienting response, which is the brain's reaction to novelty. The term was coined by Ivan Pavlov (yes, the dog and the bell Pavlov!). During the orienting response, our brain momentarily shuts down some body systems, like respiration. We cock our heads to one side to give our auditory system the best chance of locating and identifying any sounds. We orient our gaze toward the location of the novel stimulation. Our eyebrows go slightly upward to increase our visual field to the maximum. Everything else stops for an instant until we have determined if the novel stimulus is harmful or helpful.

Teachers can take advantage of the orienting response by occasionally introducing novel stimuli into the environment. During that momentary pause when the orienting response occurs, teachers can give new directions.

The skill you will learn today is how to introduce novel sounds into the classroom environment to trigger the orienting response. Our response to novel sounds is an involuntary survival mechanism. Our ancestors lived in hostile environments, and their very survival depended on their ability to immediately assess novel sounds in the environment—such as a twig breaking under the paw of a stalking predator—into their conscious awareness. Introducing novel sounds into your classroom takes advantage of this ancient reflex.

Skill: **Sound Makers**

Here's how to do it:

1 Get a collection of novel sound makers. I suggest having at least four or five in your collection. You can find novel sound makers in a variety of places: an outdoor outfitter's shop for animal calls; a science museum gift shop for interesting sound makers; a party store for New Year's Eve noisemakers. And don't forget to ask a music teacher for novel sound maker recommendations, too!

2 Choose one of the novel sound makers to use today. (For this example, I'm using a sound maker from a sporting goods store that simulates the sound a deer makes, called a deer grunt.)

3 Say to the students, "OK, students; discuss in your groups until you hear the deer grunt. When you hear the deer grunt, all conversation stops and you look at me for further instructions." They won't know what a deer grunt is, but that's the idea.

4 When you are ready to get attention back, blow on the deer grunt (it makes a low, gravelly sound). Because this is novel to the students, the orienting response gets triggered. During the brief pause when they are checking to see what the sound was, ask them to look at you, and then give them the next set of directions.

Keep your eyes out for inexpensive noisemakers. Don't use any of them too frequently. If you have a small collection, you can rotate them when you want to get the students' attention this way, and they will retain their novelty. I have a pretty big collection of noisemakers, so I try to use each novel sound only once per year, and I don't bring it back until I have a new set of students.

Another way to use a novel sound:

• Sudden Silence

The Sudden Silence uses sound in a different way to get students' attention. Students are working at their desks or working in groups. You have music playing quietly in the background. When you need the students' attention, gradually increase the volume of the music playing, and then suddenly stop the music. This sudden wall of silence is novel, and will activate the orienting response. Be ready to give your next directions as soon as you have the students' attention.

Week 2: Keeping Attention

Getting attention in the short term can be relatively easy. *Keeping* attention for extended periods of time can be really difficult some days. Students get restless and need to take a break. They can be easily distracted by anything: a voice over the loudspeaker, a knock on the door, or even the way you move around the room. If the classroom is messy or disorganized, many students have trouble maintaining focus. And even if you have established a calm atmosphere in the class, kids may need a small jolt to get back on track.

By the end of this week, you will have five skills that will help you know when students need a break, and strategies to refresh their attention and keep the learning going. You will learn how to create an environment that helps your students pay attention to what's important in the classroom.

There are five components for keeping attention in Week Two:

[**MONDAY**] Needing a Break   [**THURSDAY**] Vary the Routine

[**TUESDAY**] Taking a Break   [**FRIDAY**] Kinesthetic Learning

[**WEDNESDAY**] Eliminate Distractions

Needing a Break

I have heard teachers say, "Students can only pay attention for twenty minutes." This is simply not true. Some students can't even pay attention for *two* minutes. Some students can pay attention for much longer than twenty minutes. The difference is complicated by many factors. Is the student hungry? Tired? Did the student just break up with his girlfriend before class? Is this a subject in which the student is interested?

Here's a typical scenario in a fifth grade classroom: School starts at 8:30. For the first fifteen minutes, the students do silent reading while the teacher takes attendance, collects field trip money, and does the lunch count and other mundane but necessary tasks. At 8:45, the teacher has students get out their math books and they work on the math lesson. At about 9:15, she tells the students, "Now you can put away your math books," with audible sounds of relief from the students. And then she continues ". . . and get out your social studies books." This elicits a loud chorus of groans and sounds of pain from the students. For the next fifteen minutes, she has lost the students' attention. Not much social studies teaching happens, as the teacher constantly asks students to sit down, wait to use the bathroom, stop talking, etc.

Here's the problem with this picture: The students were sitting for 45 minutes without a break, and when they needed a break, the teacher didn't give it to them. She didn't stop because she thought a break would be wasting time.

A break is *not* wasting time! Learn to tell when your students need a break, and then give them one. Do a quick activity to regain your students' attention. You will be *investing* time to create the optimal learning environment.

How can you tell when your students need a break? Observe their physiology. The body and brain are connected. Whatever happens in the body affects the brain; whatever happens in the brain affects the body. With a little practice, you can read physiological cues that tell when your students need a break.

Today, you'll learn how to "read the class" and know when they need a break.

Skill: Read the Class

Here's how to do it:

While you are teaching today, make the conscious effort to watch when your students exhibit one or several of the following physiological cues. (Tomorrow's skill will focus on what to do when they need a break.) Note in your lesson plan book which physiological cues you saw today, how often, and at what time they occurred.

1 Fidgeting

Watch for your students moving. If you have been teaching for an extended period of time without a break (over twenty minutes or more, depending on the age of the students), watch for movements like these that indicate their attention has lapsed and it's time for a break:

* Wiggling in their seats

* Shuffling papers

* Getting up and moving around the room at inappropriate times

* Tapping their pencils or drumming their fingers

2 Talking

Listen for the hum of chitchat in your classroom or side conversations when they aren't called for. That might indicate that students simply need redirection and a reminder to pay attention, or it might be a signal that students need a break.

3 Slumping

Are your students:

* Holding their heads up with one or both hands?

* Slouching in their chairs?

* Laying their heads on their desks?

When you see a few students slumping, it's probably a signal that the class needs a break. But one note of caution: a student could be doing these behaviors to ease physical pain. f you see one particular student slumping often, that may be a different signal altogether.

4 Lack of eye contact

Check if your students are:

* Glancing at the clock or their watches

- Looking out the window or into the hallway

- Looking glassy-eyed and unfocussed

- Looking away from you

It's easy to notice when even one student has lost eye contact with you, since all of them should be looking at you when you are leading the class.

5 Lack of focus

Do your students:

- Need directions repeated?

- Ask questions about something you taught earlier?

- Have a difficult time volunteering?

- Look tired?

These kinds of behaviors may indicate that students' energy is flagging and their attention is lost. A break might be just the thing to get everyone back on track.

Take note of these physiological cues and note when they happen during the day. When the day is over, review your list to see how often the students' attention was lost. Look for patterns. Did they lose attention more at the end of the class period? More at the end of the day, or the beginning of the day? Tomorrow you can try taking a break when you notice these physiological cues.

Taking a Break

Now that you've learned how to notice when the students need a break, today you will learn how to give students a break while maintaining control of the classroom.

Students of all ages can focus attention only for a finite period of time. If students have been sitting too long and

HERE'S THE RESEARCH

The cerebellum is also connected to learning, language (Booth et al., 2007), memory (Desmond et al., 1997) and attention (Courchesne and Allen, 1997).

their bodies are getting stiff and tired, that may affect their ability to concentrate.

The part of the brain responsible for coordinating movement is the cerebellum, which means "little brain" in Latin. We need to keep the cerebellum active during learning, and movement is one of the best ways to do it. Moving stimulates learning, memory, language development, and attention.

That's why these ideas to refresh the class involve movement of some kind. When you notice that your students have lost attention and need a break, don't just stop teaching and let students have free time until you feel like they are refreshed. Keep control of the breaks to make them most effective. These break ideas are teacher-facilitated activities that give students a break in a structured way to help them get re-energized and ready for work again quickly.

Skill: Refresh the Class

Here's how to do it:

First, use your knowledge from yesterday's observations to recognize signs that your students may need a break. Then try one of the following break ideas to refresh the students. Use your judgment to decide when the short, medium, or long break will do the trick. For practice, try to use each kind of break at least once today. You may notice your students need more than three breaks today, but for now, make sure you use each type of break idea at least once a day while you're learning this skill. And when you call for the break, do it along with your students—teachers need to be re-energized, too!

1 Short Break (10 seconds)—Deep Breaths

The brain relies on a constant supply of blood to supply it with nutrients and oxygen. Not getting enough oxygen can negatively affect a child's development, behavior, and even academic achievement. Having students take a few deep breaths will help all of that!

HERE'S THE RESEARCH

Adverse effects of even mild oxygen deprivation, known as hypoxia, have been documented (Bass et al., 2004).

Have students stop what they are doing, stand up, and take a few deep breaths before beginning their work again. Tell them to breathe *in* for five counts and *out* for five counts, which you count aloud slowly. Three ins and outs is a good short break.

When they are done, have them sit back down and begin to work again.

2 Medium Break (30 seconds)—Heel Lifts

The calf muscles in your legs help keep blood moving. They work almost like a second heart, moving the blood from the legs back up to the heart. When the calf muscles are inactive, as they are when students are sitting down, there is a significant decrease in blood flow.

HERE'S THE RESEARCH

Doing a simple heel-raising exercise has been shown to increase blood flow up to seven times that of resting blood flow (Boushel et al., 2000).

When it's time for a break, have students stand up and do heel lifts for thirty seconds. They raise their heels and balance on the balls of their feet for one to two seconds, and then slowly lower their heels to the ground. Repeat this two or three times in thirty seconds or so. Lift both feet at once, one foot at a time, or any other variation. It's fun to play some fast music and invite the students to move their heels up and down to the beat. This will get oxygenated blood flowing to their brains and help them pay attention when everyone sits down again to work.

3 Long Break (2 minutes)—One-Song Break

Play a short song and let students stand up, stretch, get a drink of water, etc. I like to play songs from the Sixties—many of them are short (lots of Beatles songs are just over two minutes), have clean lyrics, and are familiar to students.

HERE'S THE RESEARCH

Playing music with an upbeat tempo has been shown to increase focus and work production (Lesiuk, 2005) and can increase blood flow to the brain, while at the same time stimulating reward centers in the brain (Blood and Zatorre, 2001).

Two elements are key to this break:

* They can't sit down while the song is playing. This encourages activation of the calf muscle pump and helps stimulate blood flow to the brain.

* They must be sitting down and ready to work when the song ends. Give them a five-second warning before the song stops so they can get in their seats.

WEEK 2

Eliminate Distractions

Another approach to keeping the attention of your students is to reduce or eliminate environmental distractions that can compete for attention. We have to combat students' distractibility and keep their attention where we want it: on the lesson! We can accomplish this in part by eliminating distractions in the environment.

When you eliminate distractions in the classroom you bring harmony to the environment. A harmonious classroom is one that is uncluttered, neat, with straight desks, window blinds pulled to the same height, and no paper or trash on the floor. Harmony in the classroom may be invisible to the students, but it is very effective for helping students pay attention longer.

HERE'S THE RESEARCH

Distracting stimuli have been shown to significantly reduce the recall of information (Shamo, 1969). Research has indicated that unless there is some way to show the importance of one stimulus over another, all stimuli are regarded equally by the observer (Theeuwes, 1991).

Some fascinating research in this area comes from research on airline pilots. When information on their displays was illuminated equally, the pilots had a more difficult time comprehending important flight information. Only when the clutter was diminished and the important information highlighted did pilot performance improve (Ververs and Wickens, 1998).

It is a culturally and biologically hard-wired characteristic of humans to survey the environment around us for potential threats (Shoemaker, 1996).

For teachers who insist that a cluttered classroom is part of their own unique "organizational style," I respectfully disagree. Your job is to teach children. Many of these children may be distracted by your "style." Reduce classroom clutter and bring harmony to the room to help your students focus and concentrate.

Skill: **Bring Harmony**

Here's how to do it:

1 Start before the students arrive this morning and look around the room to see what is out of place, out of line, or attracts your attention in any way.

2 Line up chairs and desks in a neat arrangement.

3 Pick paper and clutter up off the floor.

4 Straighten stacks of books, papers, CDs, or DVDs.

5 Move window blinds to the same level.

6 Hang posters, displays, and student work straight and evenly.

7 Move displays away from air vents so they don't flutter around.

8 Move computer cables or AV cables out of sight or organize them into bundles.

9 Make sure objects placed around the room—such as a tissue box, container with extra pencils, baskets for student work—are neat.

Starting today, when you walk into your classroom every morning, stand at the front of your room and check for harmony. Change what needs to be changed, straighten what needs to be straightened. The distractions are all potential attention magnets that can pull your students away from the teaching and learning going on in your classroom.

And there's more . . . teach the students to harmonize!

You can't keep your classroom in harmony every minute of every day. Teach your students how to bring harmony to the room. Have them look for the same nine distractions you checked for this morning. Choose a song to use exclusively when students are straightening up the classroom, and play that anchor music when students are straightening up the room. Have students do this at the end of each hour, or class period, or a couple of times a day. It will take less than thirty seconds if done frequently. This has the added benefit of students taking ownership in the maintenance of the classroom without being reminded.

After you have incorporated the idea of bringing harmony to your classroom, try a few more ways to eliminate distractions.

Clearly, It's Behind Me

Giving attention to one visual target leaves less attention available for other visual stimuli. Therefore, you want to reduce the amount of competing visual stimuli behind you while teaching. Don't teach in front of a busy bulletin board

HERE'S THE RESEARCH

We have a limited capacity for processing competing visual stimuli (Kastner et al., 1998).

or wall with posters, or with a movie or slide projected behind you. Best of all—teach in front of a blank wall. You want your students to focus on *you* if they can only pay attention to one visual stimulus at a time!

Non-compete Clause

Avoid competing auditory stimuli in the classroom. Pause music, a movie, or video when you or a student is speaking. When students focus on the teacher's voice and try to tune out background noise such as pencil sharpening, rustling papers, and moving chairs, the muscles of the inner ear contract to make the higher frequencies of the human voice easier to hear. Students with poor auditory figure-ground skills will have difficulty with this task, but keeping competing auditory stimuli to a minimum can help every student.

Don't Leave It Blank

Don't leave blank white screens projected when using slide projectors, overhead projectors, computer screens, or television screens. This can actually be painful to some students with sensitive eyesight, and it's potentially distracting to everyone.

Vary the Routine

One way we make sense of our world is by seeking, creating, and following patterns. Engage your students' attention by following a two-step process that uses the brain's natural affinity for patterns.

The first step is to consciously and deliberately create patterns of behavior in your classroom. These patterns will help create a sense of predictability. Patterns of behavior include the way students enter the room, how they line up to leave, how papers are passed out, and how work is collected, and so on.

The second step is to break the patterns. Once patterns have been established and the classroom environment is calm, you can gently break some patterns by doing something unexpected.

HERE'S THE RESEARCH

A break in the classroom pattern creates novelty that leads to increased student engagement and can even improve your students' long-term memory (King and Williams, 2009).

Skill: **Break the Pattern**

Here's how to do it:

Choose one of these three ways to vary your pattern today. You can try the others in the next few weeks.

- **Make a new "front" of the room**

   Before the students come in, move the desks to face the back or the side of the room, or set them at an angle. Essentially, you're moving the "front" of the room to a new location.

   Changing where the "front" of the room is located can be a fun break, can engage students, and can make it easier for your students to retrieve information stored in their brains.

• Change where students sit

Have your students change where they sit in the room. Do it when you are starting a new topic. Have the students pick up all of their belongings, put on some upbeat walking music, and challenge them to find a new seat as different from their current seat as possible. If they are sitting in the front, encourage them to sit in the back; if sitting on the left side of the room, now move to the right.

• Vary what time subjects are taught

Each student will have a different time in the day when he/she is at a learning peak. You may always teach math first thing in the morning when some students are not at their sharpest. Today, switch the time of day that a subject is taught. If you always teach math first thing in the morning, try reading first, and then math after lunch.

Kinesthetic Learning

Whether looking at elementary, middle school, or even medical students in college, kinesthetic learning has been shown to increase student involvement and academic performance.

Any time you can get kids up, out of their seats, and engaged in the material you are teaching, you will enhance learning.

HERE'S THE RESEARCH

Kinesthetic activities used to teach phonological awareness to elementary students at risk for reading were found to be very effective (Rule, 2006).

A study of middle school students who were identified as gifted but underachieving showed a strong preference for tactile and kinesthetic activities in the classroom (Rayneri, 2003).

Medical students who learned through active learning strategies rather than straight lecture showed significantly improved academic performance (Rao, 2001).

Skill: **Get Physical**

Here's how to do it:

Try one of these ideas today to "get physical" in your lessons. These ideas are simple but lots of fun for students. At the same time, they bring a kinesthetic component to the learning that keeps everyone's attention. Try the other ideas in the next few weeks.

- **This Side/That Side**

  Use this as a warm-up activity.

  Students are asked to make a choice between two options. For example, tell students, "If you are more of a cat lover, move to the right side of the room; more of a dog lover, move to the left side of the room." Then begin adding choices from the content of the lesson; for example: "If you are pro-gun control, move to the left of the room, if you are against gun control, move to the right of the room."

Corners

There is some prep work to this activity. Mark four corners in your room. You could mark them with signs that read A, B, C, or D, or something content-specific, such as "Democrat," "Republican," "Independent," and "Undecided." Each corner represents a choice, and students move to the corner that has their answer displayed. For example: "If you are more in line with the Republican party, go to the corner that has that sign; if you believe more in the Democratic party philosophy, move to that corner; if you are more of an Independent, please walk to that corner; if you are undecided, please go to that corner."

Human Graph

Students form a "human graph" as they move around the room to answer questions. The teacher poses three questions. Students who choose answer A line up together; answer B students line up next to answer A students; those who choose answer C line up next to the Bs. At the end of the process, the students have formed a life-sized bar graph!

Question/Answer Cards

Create sets of note cards that have a question on one card, and the answer to the question on another card. Give students a card at random. Students walk around the room to find their match and discuss.

Finger Vote

The teacher asks a question, and then asks students to hold up fingers in front of their chest to vote on the answers. For example, students hold up one finger for agree, two fingers for disagree, or thumbs up for agree, thumbs down for disagree.

Week 3: Engaging Students

You've learned how to get your students' attention and how to keep their attention. Now it's time to focus on engaging your students to involve them in what you're teaching. Engaged students are curious and interested in what is being taught. If students are engaged in the learning, they are motivated and optimistic about their ability to learn. A classroom full of engaged students should not have any classroom management issues.

When you engage your students, they feel emotions such as excitement, curiosity, intrigue, and surprise. By engaging their emotions, you'll keep them interested in the learning.

Engaging students is a fundamental teaching skill that needs to be practiced and mastered. If you take charge of learning how to engage students in your lessons, you'll all but eliminate discipline issues.

There are five components for engaging students in Week Three:

HERE'S THE RESEARCH

In some classrooms, only half the day is devoted to instruction, and the percentage of students not engaged can be from 50 to a startling 90 percent of students. The low engagement rates could be due to several factors, including the teacher's competence in managing the classroom (Hollowood et al., 1995).

There is overwhelming evidence that emotions are critically important to our every thought, decision, and response (Pert, 1997; Damasio, 1999). In the brain, the amygdala is an almond-shaped mass of neurons that both processes emotions and is involved in long-term memory formation. We know that emotionally charged memories are stored more readily than boring or neutral memories (Bloom, Beal, and Kupfer, 2002).

MONDAY Eye Contact	**THURSDAY** Variety
TUESDAY Bumpers and Teasers	**FRIDAY** Establish Context
WEDNESDAY Make It Meaningful	

WEEK 3

Eye Contact

O ne of the most under-utilized, yet easiest to implement, teaching techniques is eye contact. Called "mutual gaze" in the literature, eye contact has been shown to have numerous positive effects on learning. We are such social beings that the act of looking someone in the eyes can be a great communication and rapport-building skill.

But be careful—you must be sensitive to cultural differences. For example, in East Asian countries, including China, Korea, and Japan, eye contact with an adult or authority figure can be interpreted as rude. In those countries,

> **HERE'S THE RESEARCH**
>
> Eye contact has been shown to facilitate the encoding and subsequent recall of information (Fry and Smith, 1975) and increase students' recall of a story that was read to them (Sherwood, 1988). Research on the benefits of teacher's eye contact with students shows that it makes students more compliant, participate more, and like the instructor better (Hamlet et. al., 1984). Research has also supported the idea of teacher eye contact as a major factor in keeping students on task (Yarbrough, 1981).

children show respect for their elders by *not* making direct eye contact. Be aware of the cultural makeup of your students in case direct eye contact is an issue for your group.

For most teachers, though, making eye contact and holding a student's gaze is an immediate way to engage your students in the classroom. But since it's not a natural skill for many of us, it's important to learn it today and practice it throughout the week until you become comfortable.

Skill: **Holding the Gaze**

Here's how to do it:

Practice making eye contact while you teach a lesson you have taught before and know well. This way, you can practice making eye contact until it becomes more automatic, since you do not have to focus as much on the lesson itself.

1 Choose a lesson to teach today that you know very well.

2 As you begin to teach the lesson, start with the student at one end of the front row, and hold that student's gaze for about three seconds. Then proceed to the next student in the row and make eye contact with him/her for three seconds, and so on.

3 Continue working your way through the classroom, one student at a time, until you establish eye contact with every student for several seconds.

4 Then start over and practice making eye contact again, one by one.

At first this may feel uncomfortable or awkward, but eventually it will become second nature. You'll learn to make eye contact in a random pattern around the room and for different lengths of time.

After you've practiced holding your students' gazes for a while today, try this skill next time your students are entering your room:

- **Feeling Your Presence**

   As students enter the room, stand confidently in the front of the room, with your feet firmly planted and a welcoming smile on your face. Scan the room, smiling and making eye contact with the students until they are all in their seats and you are ready to start class. Students will "feel your presence." This behavior gives a strong message that you are confident, prepared, professional, and ready for anything. Your steady presence at the front of the room helps students focus on getting started with their work quicker, and adds a sense of control and calm to the classroom.

WEEK 3

Bumpers and Teasers

Watch any news show or listen to a radio disc jockey. Notice how they encourage the viewer to tune in to see a story later in the broadcast, or to stay tuned after the commercial break. They do it by giving what are called "bumpers" or "teasers" with just enough information to keep the viewer or listener hooked. Bumpers take place at the beginning of a broadcast, and teasers are given before a commercial break.

HERE'S THE RESEARCH

Bumpers and teasers have been shown to be very effective to encourage continued listening and to increase understanding and recall of stories (Gehrard, 1992; Chang, 1998).

Use bumpers and teasers to create curiosity. At the beginning of a class, give students part of a question that isn't answered until later. To get students curious about what's coming up next after a break or perhaps the next class, drop some hints. Do this several times a day, just before you are about to teach a new lesson and at the end of the day. Bumpers and teasers in the classroom sound something like this:

- "After lunch, we will find the two most important things that Columbus can teach us about risk taking and success in your life."

- "Tomorrow we will put 110 volts of electrical current through a mystery vegetable and watch something amazing happen. See you in the morning!"

Skill: Teaser Templates

Here's how to do it:

Start listening to newscasters on television and radio, and learn from their examples how they use bumpers and teasers to keep you tuned in and curious. Today, think about your topics, and give at least one teaser to your class using one of these nine "teaser templates." Think about what you will be teaching today, and prepare your bumper or teaser to read to the class. Decide exactly when you'll give the class the bumper or teaser. When you get the hang of using them, they will come naturally and you won't have to prepare them in advance.

The Unusual

"When we come back (after the break, tomorrow, next session), I'll tell you one (pick an adjective). . .

weird

strange

simple

little-known

unusual

. . . thing you can do that can make a big difference in your life."

The Secret

"When we come back (after the break, tomorrow, next session), I'll let you in on one of the biggest secrets to happiness and success that has ever been discovered."

The Personal Connection

"Later today, I'll tell you about a kid about your age who thought_____, and ended up thinking _____."

The Exclusive Tip

"Next time, I'll tell you the single biggest thing that successful people do to be happy."

The Celebrity Connection

"First thing in the morning, we will find out what Kanye, Beyonce, and you have in common."

The Surprising Statistic

"Tomorrow we will find out what percentage of kids your age are _____."

The Choice

"This afternoon we will discover what would be more likely to stop peer pressure: _____ or _____."

The List

"In a few minutes, we'll discuss the three most important things about . . ."

● The Unbelievable but True

"In the next lesson, you will learn something that will blow your mind . . ."

Make It Meaningful

WEEK 3
W

When you learn rote information, such as multiplication facts or a list of helping verbs, those facts are stored in the brain in isolation. There is no meaning associated with the learning of facts when they are taught by rote. Students often "learn" this way without real understanding or associating any meaning with the information.

But meaningful information in our brain is connected to other information. The action of recall activates different neural networks in our brain, for a more comprehensive, rich, and complete reconstruction and comprehension of the material.

HERE'S THE RESEARCH

When concepts are learned in a meaningful way, "spreading activation" occurs (Anderson, 1983; Crestani, 1997).

Research shows that engagement goes up when students are told why they are learning the information, and if the teacher suggests how the new learning may be related to events or experiences in their lives (Gettinger and Seibert 2002).

When the information you are teaching is meaningful and relevant to your students, they will learn it on a more profound level. Make it meaningful!

Skill: Bringing It Home

Here's how to do it:

Try one of these three ideas today to help make your teaching meaningful to your students.

Real Life

Tell your students how the information you are teaching benefits them. Show students practical examples of how they can use the material in their own lives. For example, if you are teaching an economics lesson about wages, have your students calculate how many hours they would have to work making minimum wage to make what an NBA player makes in one game.

Past, Present, or Future

Tell the students how this lesson connects to events in their past, experiences in their present, or possibilities in their future. Show students how the information being taught connects to other topics or other subjects.

Journals

Writing in journals can help students find meaning in their learning. Pose higher-level questions to your students and have them write answers in a journal. There are two ways to do this, depending on the age of your students:

a. If your students are middle school-aged or younger, ask an open-ended question about your topic and have them write about it. For example, for teachers of middle school math, a question could be, "How do we use math in our daily lives?" Let students write in their journals for about five minutes, thinking of ways that they use math every day. Afterwards, you can ask students to volunteer to share their ideas.

B. For older students, try a more structured approach: the Double Entry Journal (Millis and Cottell, 1998). Students make a T-chart on a piece of paper. They write down key words, phrases, and critical ideas from the lesson on the left side of the chart. On the right side, they write a response to the left side, addressing their reaction, feelings, questions they may still have, connections they made, etc.

Variety

The lecture format is a popular way for teachers to relay information. It works well to cover a lot of material quickly. But it's not the only way. Lecturing is not inherently bad, but if you only teach through lectures you are not connecting with students who have different learning styles.

To keep students interested and engaged, use a variety of methods and media when teaching. If you discover that weeks have gone by, and all you have done is the lecture/worksheet/homework format, you need to challenge yourself to add some variety to your teaching methods.

The magic formula for engagement seems to be a mixture of autonomy support and structure. Autonomy support is the teacher's interaction with students about their interests and teachers' efforts to develop and nurture those interests. Teacher behaviors that increase autonomy support include seeking out and accepting students' thoughts, feelings, and perspectives, and giving time for all students to make sense of the material. The second part is structure. If the teacher is having students participate in a fun, structured activity that elicits their thoughts, feelings, and perspectives about the material at hand, engagement will occur.

Today, incorporate the activity Rank Order into your activities to increase engagement with your students.

HERE'S THE RESEARCH

A study of nearly 1,800 faculty members at five different types of institutions found that, regardless of institutional type (large or small, public or independent, community college or research university), 73 to 83 percent of respondents indicated that the lecture was their main instructional method, used more than discussion, recitation, lab/shop, applied instruction (in music), and individualized instruction (Blackburn et al. 1980).

In 1977, a meta-analysis concluded that students learn more from reading complex material than they do from lectures about the same material (Davis and Alexander, 1977).

Researchers have learned about the importance of autonomy support (Jang, Reeve, and Deci, 2010).

Skill: **Rank Order**

Here's how to do it:

1 To play Rank Order, first choose your topic. For this example, we'll use the topic: "What is the most important problem facing schools today?"

2 List possible answers on the board, such as: standardized testing, school uniforms, guns in school, school security, and school funding.

3 In groups of four to six, ask students to rank order the problems from most important problem to least important. They can do this alone or with a partner.

When you play Rank Order, you can ask students to rank ideas in terms of most important, hardest to remember, most likely to be on the test, or any number of other metrics.

The actual order the students come up with is relatively unimportant. What is important is the process of dialogue and debate that comes with developing the rank order, which makes meaning of the information.

In the next few weeks, try some of these ideas to add variety to your teaching:

- **Demonstration**
  As an example, if you are introducing the commutative property in math, have students get involved in a demonstration. Have three groups of four students stand inside Hula-Hoops to demonstrate 3 x 4 = 12, and then have the same students group themselves in four groups of three students to show 4 x 3 = 12.

- **Experiment**
  Students develop a hypothesis before the experiment begins, and gather data to see if the hypothesis was correct. This, of course, works perfectly when you're teaching science. For example, when teaching about freezing points, set out two ice cubes. Have students guess how salt will affect the melting of the ice cubes, then sprinkle salt on top of one ice cube and leave the other untouched.

- **Compare and contrast**
  Have students identify similarities and differences between two concepts.

- **Opinion poll**
  Have students stand up if they agree with a statement you make. For example, the teacher can say, "Stand up if you believe that Abraham Lincoln was our greatest president." Then you have the opportunity to talk about what he did to justify that opinion (or not).

● Sample

Pass around a sample or representation of what the lesson is about. If you are studying the difference between igneous and sedimentary rocks, pass some samples around while you discuss, or have samples at the table for students to touch and examine to make the lesson come to life.

● Role-play

Have students create a situation and role-play it for the class. If you are studying conflict resolution in a life skills class, the students could role-play a good way to handle a conflict, as well as a way that is not effective.

● New blood!

Bring in a guest speaker.

● Drama

Have students create a skit. I am always surprised how many students enjoy creating skits and performing them for the class. Make one option for an assignment to have students create and perform a skit that illustrates the points you are studying.

● Pecha Kucha

Try a Pecha Kucha (Japanese for "chatter") presentation. Show 20 slides, each for 20 seconds, for a total of 6 minutes and 40 seconds for the presentation. It's a great way to organize your PowerPoint presentation so your students keep their attention. Or have your students create their presentations in this style. See www.rethinkpresentations.com/the-art-of-pecha-kucha for an example and explanation.

WEEK 3

F

Establish Context

Putting information into a larger context can help engage students with the material. We need to know individual facts, but without the big picture in which to place them, they can be useless.

The brain is divided into two hemispheres with specialized functions. The left hemisphere processes sequences, facts, and parts. The right hemisphere is more abstract, holistic, and conceptual. To understand a concept, one must have both the details and the bigger context in which the details fit.

Give the students the big picture. Show them where all the information they are learning fits in to the grand scheme of the lesson, the class, or the semester. Teaching is most effective when students can see where the parts fit into the whole. Introduce and organize new material in terms of natural wholes, such as projects, stories, and big ideas.

Skill: The Big Picture

Here's how to do it:

Today, try one of these ideas to help give your class the big picture. Select the one that will work best for your age group and for the material you are currently teaching. You can try other ideas as the year goes along.

- **"You are here" map**

  This technique shows students where the current topic fits into the timeline of the semester. Think of it like the map in a shopping mall with the big red dot that says, "You are here."

  Create a timeline of the major events, activities, or topics in the material. Show the timeline today, and using a bingo chip as the dot, demonstrate that they are starting something new. Then pull out the timeline at appropriate times and move the dot forward to show students the progress they have made through the topic, and how much longer they have to go until it is completed.

- **Syllabus**

  In middle or high school, a complete syllabus that shows all major topics, essential understandings for the course, assignments, due dates, rubrics, grading scale, and skills to be learned is a great resource for students. It clearly shows students the big picture for the semester or for the topic to be learned.

- **Curriculum map**

  A curriculum map shows the major topics arranged by month or by week at the approximate dates when they will be introduced. The map for a semester-long class would show the months and map the units of study by approximately how long each will take. For example, to teach a US history course, the Civil War may be mapped as being studied through September and October, and Reconstruction would then be studied in November. This idea works well for students of all ages.

- **Graphic organizer**

  Show the connection between all of the content progress of the class with a graphic organizer. For example, if you are teaching geometry, use a graphic organizer that has the word "area" in the middle and then in branches off that word, show all the different geometric figures for which you will be learning to calculate the area: triangle, square, rectangle, circle, etc.

Week 4: Teaching the Lesson

Students today are inundated with an enormous amount of information, and it seems to be growing every year. How does the brain adjust to this ever-growing mountain of information?

Simple—it rewires itself. The neuroplasticity of the brain allows it to change as a result of interaction with the environment. The brains of students today look the same and have the same structures and functions as brains of students in decades past, but are wired differently in some fundamental and profound ways.

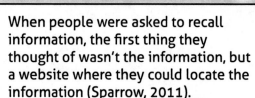

HERE'S THE RESEARCH

When people were asked to recall information, the first thing they thought of wasn't the information, but a website where they could locate the information (Sparrow, 2011).

Research shows that using effective teaching techniques can reduce the number of incidents of students acting out by as much as 44 percent (Ford et al., 2001).

Today, students are more likely to remember the *source* of information and where we can find it, rather than the information itself. Since students expect to be able to find information later, brains seem to put less effort into getting the information into long-term storage.

With so much information washing over our students, and with students' brains wired more for *searching* information than *storing* it, educators have a challenge. How can we help bring the information to the forefront of students' focus so that our curriculum doesn't get lost in the landslide of information? What can we do to help students create the structures of information in their brains so they can connect disparate pieces of information in their minds to create new ideas and comprehend larger concepts? What skills can we give our students to help them manage large amounts of information?

This week's skills are designed to help teachers teach to this rewired brain of the new millennia. They help with both teaching and classroom management.

There are five components for teaching the lesson in Week Four:

MONDAY Prepare to Learn   **THURSDAY** Chunking

TUESDAY Clear Communication   **FRIDAY** Review

WEDNESDAY Gestures

WEEK 4
M

Prepare to Learn

When we begin to learn something new, the brain creates a "rough draft" of the information. This rough draft is the beginning of a schema that organizes the information. Each time the information is revisited, reviewed, or re-experienced, details are added to the rough draft. Eventually, a schema or structure is created that organizes related ideas and provides a framework for us to understand new information about the topic.

HERE'S THE RESEARCH

The lack of schema may explain why so many educational trends, such as discovery, constructivist, problem-based, experiential, and inquiry-based learning do not work as well as it was originally hoped they would (Kirschner, 2006).

To prepare students for learning and to help them develop this schema of knowledge in their brains, the first step is to bring to their conscious awareness any previous knowledge, experience, or memories the students may have of the upcoming topic. Until the students have enough schema to solve the problems on their own, the teacher must be more of a direct guide in their learning.

Today, when you introduce a new topic to your students, first activate their existing schema by brainstorming what they may already know about the topic. This will get your students prepared to learn new material.

Skill: Brainstorming

Here's how to do it:

Before beginning a new topic, try brainstorming to get students ready to learn.

1 On the board at the front of the room, write the topic in the center and put a circle around it.

2 Have a student at the board as the scribe.

3 With you facilitating, ask students to share anything they know about the topic—facts, figures, stories related to the topic, videos they have seen, books they have read, news stories they have watched, etc.

4 The student scribe records all comments on the board so everyone can see them.

After you've been successful with brainstormng, try other ideas to help students prepare to learn:

- **AWL chart (Already Know/Want to Know/Learned)**

  Students create three lists: what they already know about the topic, what they want to know, and at the end of the unit, what they have learned.

- **TTYN (Turn to Your Neighbor)**

  Students turn to the student sitting next to him/her and share what they know about the topic.

- **Story or video**

  The teacher reads a story or shows a video clip related to the topic.

- **Pre-lesson check-in**

  List on poster paper the major topics that will be shared in that lesson and have students put a check mark on the topics with which they are familiar.

- **New Vocabulary**

  Read and display new vocabulary words to students before they are introduced. When students encounter the vocabulary during the lesson, they will be ready to understand the concepts.

- **Pre-exposure**

  Give students some information about the topic before you start to teach it. For example: if the unit you will teach next week is about whales, start creating an environment in the classroom that is filled with whales. Put up pictures of whales, have books in the room about whales, have stuffed whales placed around the room. Your students will know what's coming next and their brains will start thinking about the new topic.

Clear Communication

One way to help students focus on what information is important is simply to tell them.

Be absolutely clear what you want your students to learn. Don't keep it a secret. Post the learning objective in the classroom. At every logical opportunity, inform the students what they are learning and why they are learning it. Tell the students at the beginning of the lesson what the lesson will be about, and then ask them at the end if they got it. Make sure the students know *what* they are doing, and *why* they are doing it.

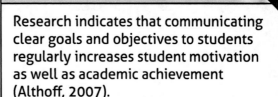

HERE'S THE RESEARCH

Research indicates that communicating clear goals and objectives to students regularly increases student motivation as well as academic achievement (Althoff, 2007).

Skill: One-Point Lesson Plan

Here's how to do it:

1. Determine the one learning objective for your lesson. You may have more than one, but distill your lesson to its essence for this purpose.

2. Post that learning objective on the board. It should reflect what the students should know or be able to do by the end of your lesson.

3. Before the lesson begins, have the students read the learning objective aloud together.

4. At least once during the lesson, remind the students about the learning objective and why they are learning this material.

4. At the end of the lesson, do a quick formative assessment to check if the students achieved the objective. This could be something as simple as having each student turn to a neighbor and explain the major point of the lesson.

When you are comfortable with the one-point lesson plan, extend it to your whole day. Write an agenda on the board that lists the activities for the day. Instead of subject areas (Math, Science, etc.), write the learning objective:

Math: "Double digit times double digit multiplication"
Science: "The four parts of the water cycle"

Use those learning objectives to guide your one-point lesson plans all day.

WEEK 4

Gestures

In 1967, Albert Mehrabian did ground-breaking research on nonverbal communication. He was the first to show quantitatively that the majority of all interpersonal communication is in the form of nonverbal messages. Your gestures are far more important than you may think.

Here's an example of how gestures can help students learn: In one study (Goldin-Meadow, 2001), children in the control group were taught a math problem without using gestures. The problem was 6 + 3 + 4 = ____ + 4. The students were taught to say

HERE'S THE RESEARCH

Many studies have indicated the importance of clear gestures (Lewis, 2000; Singer, 2005; Goldin-Meadow, 2009).

Teachers' gestures have been shown to help students learn in a variety of subjects (Crowder, 1996).

Gesturing has been shown to improve spatial working memory and speech production (Morsella, 2004).

the following words: "I want to make one side equal to the other side." The experimental group was shown the same problem and taught the same script, but they were also taught to use the following gestures: point to "6 + 3" with two fingers of the left hand, and then point to the blank with the right index finger. The gesture helped students see that if the two numbers (6 + 3) are added together, their sum is the one number that belongs in the blank.

Whenever possible, your gestures should reinforce the concepts being taught.

Using gestures effectively can also be a technique to help students with specific learning disabilities.

Today's skill will help you make your gestures a powerful teaching tool.

Skill: Use Your Hands

Here's how to do it:

1 Select one topic you will be teaching today. Think about how you will talk about the concept.

2 Develop specific gestures to use as you summarize the most important parts of the concept. Make sure the gestures aren't random hand movements. Develop movements that bring to life the words you are saying. For example, if you are talking about the life cycle of a frog, make a circle when you say the word "cycle." Make swimming motions with your hands as you talk about tadpoles, etc.

3 Create and use at least five distinct gestures for teaching today's topic.

4 Get the students involved in the gesturing. Tell them the benefits of gesturing and have them come up with their own to share with the class. They will always surprise you.

HALLWAY REVIEW

If you have some down time in school (waiting for an assembly to start or waiting in line to get into the cafeteria with your class), use that time to review the lessons you have learned with your students. During your quick hallway review, make sure to incorporate the gestures you used originally during the lesson to help teach the concepts to the students. The gestures will reinforce what the students have learned.

WEEK 4
Th

Chunking

The human memory has limits.

For example, what if you had to memorize the following list of letters?

TWANBCJFKCIANBAATM

Memorizing that list would be very difficult, but if you arrange the same information into chunks that make sense, it's much easier on the student. You can chunk the letters this way:

TWA   NBC   JFK   CIA   NBA   ATM

This is the same information, just chunked differently. It will only take a few minutes to memorize the string of letters when they are chunked.

There are many examples of this in our world. Phone numbers are seven digits long; zip codes consist of five digits. Social security numbers are nine digits long, arranged in three chunks to help us remember them.

Today you'll organize your material into logical chunks to help students learn.

> **HERE'S THE RESEARCH**
>
> In general, humans can remember seven chunks of information, plus or minus two chunks (Miller, 1956).

Skill: Break It Down

Here's how to do it:

1 Take a look at the information you are teaching. Are there natural breaks in the information? Maybe there are steps in a process you are teaching, or an introduction, followed by groups of facts. Find a reasonable chunk, teach it, then stop and review.

2 If you cannot find a chunk that makes sense, use a clock. Teach for a half hour, and then stop to review.

3 Count down the chunks as you teach. Hold up three fingers and say, "This is the third point; only two more to go (and hold up two fingers)!"

4 Make sure you review each chunk before moving on to new material.

When you're comfortable with the concept of chunking as a teaching strategy, try scaffolding:

• Scaffolding

Scaffolding is close companion to chunking. It's a way of providing support to the students when they aren't ready to learn the entire concept. Think of scaffolding as "pitching it where they can hit it." For example, if students are struggling with subtraction problems that need regrouping, you may scaffold the task by having students first identify which problems may need regrouping. This is another way of chunking information—putting it into bites small enough for students to experience success.

WEEK 4

Review

As soon as we learn information, the memory of it starts to decay (Thorndike, 1914). Teachers need to occasionally take a break to review or reflect on the learning so far. Stop after teaching a chunk of information and have students review the information. This will give you feedback on the accuracy of the information that that they are storing. One or two times per hour is ideal.

An important distinction must be made. Simply reviewing the information verbally will not create a strong memory trace and is not effective in transferring information into long-term memory. Review can benefit long-term memory production if it involves deeper thinking skills, such as thinking about the meaning of the information, and connecting the new information to information already stored.

Today you'll begin to experience the power of reviewing. Try the Teach It! strategy. It needs no advance preparation.

HERE'S THE RESEARCH

Timely feedback has been shown to greatly increase retention. In one study, participants were asked to learn foreign words. After a one-week interval, students were retested. Students who were immediately given the correct answer after an incorrect answer during review sessions in class had retention of almost 500 percent over those who did not receive corrective feedback immediately after an incorrect answer (Pashler et al., 2005).

Skill: Teach It!

Here's how to do it:

1 First, teach a chunk of information, stopping when there is a natural break before you go on to new information.

2 Have students stand up and find a partner.

3 While they are standing, give each partner thirty seconds to reteach to their partner what they just learned from the teacher.

4 After thirty seconds, announce that the other partner should now teach what they learned.

5 When the second partner is done, instruct the students to give each other a high five, say "thank you very much" to their partners, and return to their seats.

After you have used Teach It! successfully, try these other review strategies:

- **"I Know I Got It!"**
  Compile a list of the information students should know about a topic into an "I Know I Got It!" sheet. Students review the list by themselves or with a partner to make sure that they know and understand the information. Students mark a check next to each item when they feel confident that they comprehend that piece of information. Give time for questions and answers.

- **Graphic organizer**
  Have students organize the information they just learned in a graphic organizer, such as a Venn diagram or mind map.

- **Dartboard review**
  List all the major topics the students need to review on a large numbered list posted on a metal surface. Then throw a magnetic dart at the list. The number the dart lands on is the topic that students review first.

- **Ping-pong review**
  Use twenty-five ping-pong balls. Number each ball 1 to 25 with a permanent marker. Create a numbered list of review topics, vocabulary words, etc. and give the list to your students. Using the same number of balls as there are review topics, release the balls on the floor in the middle of the room. Have your students grab a predetermined number of balls. Then the students review the corresponding numbered topics with a partner.

- **Elevator speech**
  Each student prepares a ten- to fifteen-second speech about something that was recently taught. (Ten to fifteen seconds is about how long you would talk to someone during a ride in an elevator.) Students pair up with an "elevator buddy" and give their speeches to each other. You could also have each student give his/her speech in front of the whole class; this way, you'll see if their short summaries indicate their understanding of the subject.

• Jenga® Review

In the game Jenga®, small blocks of wood are stacked into a tower. In turn, each player removes one block until the tower falls. The player who causes the tower to topple loses the game. To use the game for review, write numbers on the game blocks and create a corresponding numbered review sheet. As each student removes a block, he/she checks the number and then answers the corresponding question. This works best in small groups of four students.

REPETITION

While you are teaching, after every important point, make sure to have the students repeat the key information aloud. For example, you say, "We just learned there are two ways to find our way around the globe, longitude and latitude. What are the two ways to find our way around the globe?" Students answer, "Longitude and latitude."

START HOMEWORK IN CLASS

Near the end of class, do one or two of the homework problems on the board or have the students start one or two before they leave to make sure they are on the right track.

Week 5: Getting Participation

When students are actively participating in class, there are many wonderful benefits. For the student, participating in class makes the lesson more interesting.

There are benefits to class participation for the teacher, too. When students participate in class, the teacher gets great feedback about what students understand and what concepts may need to be re-taught. Encouraging more student participation is an important way for teachers to take charge of the management of their classrooms.

With all its benefits, why are some students still reluctant to participate? There could be several reasons:

HERE'S THE RESEARCH

If students participate in class discussions, their understanding of the concepts being studied increases (Smith et al., 2009).

Giving students an opportunity to participate and involving them in class discussions can help reduce behavioral problems, even in students with emotional and behavioral disorders (Sutherland and Wehby, 2001).

Males participate more in verbal discussions in class, and females tend to write posts more in online discussions (Caspi, Chajut, and Saporta, 2008).

- Participating in class is a risky move for many students. Answering a question posed by the teacher opens a student up to be wrong.

- Some students think that asking a question in class will make classmates think they are not smart.

- It might not be considered "cool" to look so interested in what's going on in the classroom.

- Some students are more reflective learners and prefer to think things through privately; others are naturally more outgoing and process information aloud.

- Gender plays a role in class participation.

That's a lot to combat to get students to participate! This week you'll learn skills that help create a classroom atmosphere that encourages participation and risk-taking. This week's skills also help lessen your students' embarrassment or confusion, both of which discourage students from participating.

There are five components for getting participation in Week Five:

MONDAY	Recognition		THURSDAY	Greeting
TUESDAY	Student Interaction		FRIDAY	Questions
WEDNESDAY	Lowering the Risk			

Recognition

WEEK 5

M

It is wonderful for a teacher to catch a student doing something right and give praise to that student. But if *you* (the teacher) are the only one praising students, you are missing many opportunities for positive reinforcement.

Create an atmosphere of mutual and constant support in your classroom. Involve all your students in giving recognition for the effort that everyone makes during class. You must constantly and consistently cultivate this positive, accepting atmosphere in the classroom over a number of weeks for it to become a habit with your students.

HERE'S THE RESEARCH

Research has shown:

- disruptive students generally get more negative interactions with the teacher

- the teacher is more likely to reprimand inappropriate behavior than to praise a student's positive behavior

- disruptive students tend to monopolize a disproportionately large amount of the teacher's time (Mayer and Sulzer-Azaroff, 2002).

It's natural to praise students who are doing what they should be doing. It is more difficult to praise chronically disruptive students. This is a cycle of behavior that you'll want to break, starting today.

Begin by encouraging all your students to acknowledge the efforts of their classmates. Acknowledgments happen in three ways: from the group to an individual, from group members to other group members, and from one individual to another. Try all three of these acknowledgments today.

Skill: Acknowledge the Effort

Here's how to do it:

1 **Acknowledgments from the group to an individual:**

a. When a student answers a question in class, immediately ask the class to acknowledge that effort with finger snaps.

b. You facilitate this by saying, "Thanks for the answer. Class, let's give her some finger snaps!"

c. While you enthusiastically model finger snaps in the front of the room, the entire class does finger snaps with both hands for one to two seconds before you call on the next person to answer a question.

You can have the class give finger snaps after every answer. If there are several answers to a question, announce that acknowledgments will be shared when all of the answers have been given. Then ask for a shower of finger snaps for all those who participated.

2. Acknowledgments from group members to other group members:

a. When students finish a task in a small group, have them turn to all of the other members in the group and give an acknowledgment to everyone in the group. A high-five or fist bump is an easy way for students to acknowledge each other.

b. Have students say something encouraging along with the motion. For example, tell students to give a high-five and say "Good job!" This is a great way to facilitate getting some positive words in the classroom.

c. Experiment with various words or phrases that students can use to acknowledge their group members. For example: "Turn to your partner, give him a high-five and say, "You're a genius!" or "Turn to your partner, give her a fist bump, and say, "You rock!"

3. Acknowledgments from one individual to another:

a. Every time partners complete a task, facilitate an acknowledgment between the two students. Do this by announcing to the class, "Turn to your partner, give a high-five, and say, 'Thank you very much!'"

Over time, come up with your own fun class acknowledgments. Special slogans and hand motions that your class develops to acknowledge everyone's participation will bring real ownership of this idea to your students.

WEEK 5

Student Interaction

Human beings are social animals. We are hard-wired from birth for connection and social interaction.

Research findings indicate what teachers know to be true: facilitating more social interaction in the classroom will increase the amount of learning that takes place. Teachers should allow social interaction among students for a significant part of their instruction.

A key to facilitating social interaction is establishing a balance between whole-class instruction and small-group interaction. Whole-class instruction can increase participation because the teacher can monitor the entire class and facilitate active responding from all students. But there won't be opportunities for all students to participate, and

HERE'S THE RESEARCH

In animal studies, lack of consistent socialization in young animals manifests itself in drastic, long-lasting effects on behavior, increased reaction to stressful situations and fearful behavior (Caldji et al., 1998; Francis et al., 1999; Huot et al., 2001), and in anxiety and poor emotional regulation (Mitra et al., 2005).

In orphanages where caretakers change at every shift and often have many children in their care, the lack of socialization is devastating. Orphans studied tended to also show more anxiety and cognitive emotional problems even into adulthood (Ellis et al., 2004; Van Ijzendoorn, 2006).

the level of difficulty may be too high for some students to be successful. While small-group work takes care of these issues, it may not be the most efficient use of classroom time.

Today's skill gives you two different ways to get students interacting effectively during class.

Skill: **Bring Them Together**

Here's how to do it:

Try one technique today and the other later this week.

1 Peer Tutoring

a. Pair up students and have them teach or re-teach to each other the content being learned or the content that was just taught. Choose appropriate content that is not too difficult.

HERE'S THE RESEARCH

Peer tutoring has long been known to have great benefits for the students being tutored, (Damon, 1984) and also for the one doing the tutoring (Dineen et al., 1977).

b. Monitor the pairs closely to make sure they stay on task.

When doing a partner activity such as peer tutoring, try pairing students in different ways, such as:

a. Have students partner with the classmate who sits next to, in front, or diagonally across from him/her.

b. Have students partner with a classmate who has the same attributes, such as the same color hair, the same birthday month, or the same shoe size.

2 We Agree!

a. Create student groups of three to five students.

b. Pose a controversial question; for example: "What is the one thing that could change in schools to make them better?" This can be done with actual content from the lesson you are teaching, or as a warm up exercise, with the goal to get students interacting.

c. Give groups five minutes to debate the question and come up with one answer from the group.

d. Each group picks a spokesperson. That person reports the group's answer.

There are many ways to mix groups of students. A couple of easy ones:

* Give students numbers 1 through 4, and group the 1s together, the 2s, etc.

* Put each student's name on a Popsicle stick and randomly pull the number of sticks for each group.

GROUPING STUDENTS

When putting students into groups, consider moving students around once in a while so that they are not with their usual group of friends. This will help create heterogeneous groupings for activities and discussions.

Lowering the Risk

For many students, answering a question or participating in a class activity may be too risky. They may not want to answer a question during a class discussion because they don't know if their answer is what the teacher is looking for, or they think they will look stupid in front of their friends if they make a comment that is off the point. They may be reluctant to do a physical activity in class because they may feel that they are uncoordinated, or may be unsure if they will be able to do the activity correctly or as well as their classmates.

To help overcome this reluctance, design activities that are low risk. It's similar to how animal experts train whales to jump over a rope. At first, they keep the activity so low risk that the whale is guaranteed success. Training starts by putting the rope under the surface of the water. Every time the whale swims over the rope (they were swimming anyway, so it's a very low risk), the whale is rewarded with food. The rope is raised a little bit higher each time until the whale is leaping out of the water to clear the rope. The risk factor is very low at the start, and kept low throughout the training so the whale continues to learn.

To get as many students participating as possible, you need to see the activity through the eyes of your students. If you think the activity is too risky, dial down the risk factor to make it easier on the students.

Today, try one of these ideas to lower risk: the first will get more participation in a class discussion, and the second will increase participation in a physical activity.

Skill: Lower Risk in Class Discussions

Here's how you do it:

Try this three-step process. It gives the student a "dress rehearsal" of the answer before responding in front of the whole class.

1 Pose a question to the class. Before any student answers, give some examples and sample answers. For example, you might say, "In your groups, please think of three reasons for the cause of World War Two. Think of social issues, lingering border issues left over from World War One, or even economic issues in Europe at the time."

2 Break the class into small groups or pairs so students can discuss the information first in that lower-risk format. This can be as simple as saying "Turn to the student sitting next to you and discuss your answer to the question."

3 After students have had sufficient time to discuss in the smaller groups or pairs, pause the discussion, have students give their group or partner an acknowledgment, and then bring their attention back to you. Now encourage individual students to share what they discussed with the whole class.

Make sure to have the entire class enthusiastically acknowledge (with finger snaps) the effort it took for every student who answers individually.

Skill: Lower Risk in Physical Activity

Here's how you do it:

Simplify the activity.

- If the activity involves moving around the room and some students are reluctant to participate, let them stand in place to do the activity.
- If the activity involves moving arms and hands, adapt the movement so they are only moving their hands.
- If the activity calls for switching sides of the room, have students stay on the same side of the room.
- If the activity involves crossing the midline of the body, make the activity all on the same side of the body.

ACTIVITY PLANNING

When you are planning a new unit, write each activity you plan to use on a 3 x 5 note card. Arrange the cards in front of you from the least risky activity on the left to the most risky on the right. Put the activities in order in your lesson plan book with the least risky activities first and the activities with more risk later, as students become more confident.

GROUP UP!

You can lower the risk factor of any individual activity by doing it in a group. Try this when you want your students to give presentations. Most students will be more comfortable presenting as part of a group rather than going alone.

Greeting

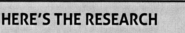
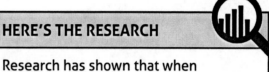

WEEK 5

Th

To help get students into a better state of mind for learning, try greeting each student individually as they come into your classroom or back from a break. This models good social protocols and can help with on-task behavior.

The greeting is a teacher-directed, pre-session behavior that can help increase student participation and decrease off-task or disruptive behaviors.

> ### HERE'S THE RESEARCH
>
> Research has shown that when teachers greeted their students as the students entered the classroom, on-task behavior in the first ten minutes of class increased from 45 percent to 72 percent of students (Allday, 2007). Teacher greeting also got students to begin tasks more quickly (Allday, 2011). Other research has found that giving attention to students before class starts reduces the amount of off-task or problem behaviors during class (McComas et. al., 2003).

Skill: Welcome Wagon

Here's how to do it:

Try any of the following ways today to greet your students. Choose one that fits your personal style, comfort zone, and the ages of the students you teach.

* Simply greet each student at the door with a friendly "Good morning!"

* Greet each student at the door with a secret, class-only handshake of their own creation.

* Greet students with their choice of a handshake, a fist bump, or a high five.

* Greet each student, and then ask each one what the daily weather is. Students respond either "sunny," "partly cloudy," or "stormy," depending on their mood.

* Greet each student at the door and ask each one how ready he/she is to learn today. Students answer by holding up their fingers. Holding up five fingers means very ready; a closed fist indicates that the student has

a lot going to deal with before he/she is in an optimal state for learning.

Make sure to greet every student in your class, not just the ones that you like: say good morning to *everyone*.

Questions

Teachers ask questions regularly of students. Sometimes teachers ask broad questions, such as "Do you all understand?" or "Does anyone have any questions?" These questions are not very effective in eliciting student responses of any kind. Even if a student does have questions or does not understand the concept being taught, it is a rare student who will raise a hand and ask for clarification.

Many questions go unanswered. Why are there so many students who do not answer questions?

Perhaps it is the teacher. Some teachers are uncomfortable with silence after they ask a question. They immediately call on another student whom they think will have an answer. This further discourages students from answering because they know that if they wait, the teacher will break down and ask someone else!

HERE'S THE RESEARCH

In a study of student responses to teacher questions, of the approximately 200 questions asked by the teacher during a 50-minute period, there was no response to 41 percent of the questions asked (White et al., 1991).

Perhaps it is the student. Maybe the student didn't have enough time to formulate an answer, or the question was multi-layered and complex, so the student didn't know exactly how to answer, or wasn't sure what the teacher was asking. The student might have been afraid of giving the wrong answer.

To encourage better class participation, you need to find ways to get everyone in your class willing to answer questions. There are two approaches: you can change the way you ask questions, and you can also add to your students' methods for answering the questions you pose. Today, try both.

Skill: Ask and Answer

Try at least one idea for how the teacher asks questions and another for how students answer questions. Try others in the coming weeks.

Here's how to do it:

Teacher Asking Questions:

- Ask students a question with a definite answer, not an open-ended question. This may not encourage higher-order thinking skills, but it will increase participation.

- Many high schools allow students to carry cell phones with them during the day. As soon as students walk in, send them a question via text blast to their cell phones, and have them respond using one of the several programs now available, such as www.remind101.com.

- Don't ask questions that require students to respond with data or content. Rather, give a statement, have students discuss the statement, and have them respond if they agree or disagree with the statement. This idea was espoused by researcher James T. Dillon (1988). For example, instead of asking "Why do you think that Germany was not satisfied with the boundaries of their country after World War Two?" make this statement: "After World War Two, the German people were satisfied with the redrawn boundaries of their country," and ask students to discuss, then agree or disagree.

Students Answering Questions:

- Don't let *anyone* in class raise a hand to answer a question. Use random selection to call on students to answer questions. Draw Popsicle sticks marked with the students' names to call on students at random, or try a randomization program from the Internet such as www.transum.org/software/RandomStudents. Random selection programs are usually included in interactive white board software. There are smartphone apps for randomly choosing students, too.

SIGNALS

If you have a student who has difficulty answering due to a specific learning disability or speech processing issue, tell him/her that you will only ask that student a question if you give a signal. For example, if you walk by the student and put a hand on his/her desk, the next question will be that student's.

- Use electronic classroom response systems, popularly known as "clickers." This is a system where each student has a hand-held "clicker," and students respond wirelessly to the questions posed by the teacher on the interactive white board by pressing the key on the clicker that corresponds to the correct answer. There is some preparation on the teacher's part before using these, and they are not always readily available due to cost, but I have seen them used very effectively to engage students.

- Give all students three 3 x 5 note cards—one red, one yellow, one green. Ask a question, and students hold up a card for their answer:

  Red card = disagree
  Green card = agree
  Yellow card = not sure or need more information.

  This lowers the risk of answering questions.

- Have students use response cards to write down and show an answer. The teacher poses the question, students write their answers on a hand-held white board, slate, or laminated card, and hold it up towards you to view. This works well with multiple-choice answers, so you can quickly check one letter on each student's board.

HERE'S THE RESEARCH

The use of response cards has been shown to increase student participation by up to fourteen percent (Gardner, Heward, and Grossi, 1994). Response cards have been shown to increase grades on quizzes and tests, and were preferred in 19 out of 20 students in one study (Narayan et al., 1990).

IT'S OK TO BE WRONG
If your students fear giving a wrong answer, you may need to explain the virtue of a wrong answer—the thinking it exposes and the possibilities for learning that it opens. Neuroscience research has shown that making a mistake, as long as it is immediately followed up by corrective feedback, is better for learning and recall (Huelser and Metcalfe, 2012).

Week 6: Giving Directions

Teachers give directions to students all day long—how to start a task, how to stop a task, how to move from one task to another. Poorly given directions can cause more problems with classroom management than almost anything else a teacher does.

Have you ever tried to put together a piece of furniture using instructions that did not make sense to you? The result: you get frustrated, angry, and it comes out wrong! The same applies in a classroom. The teacher knows exactly what the students need to do, but the directions don't work.

There are students who have difficulty paying attention and didn't hear the directions when you gave them. There are students who have trouble processing auditory information and need more time to assimilate the information.

When students are unclear about directions, they often act out rather than admit that they didn't hear or understand the directions. Giving clear, concise directions that mobilize students and make events happen in the classroom helps create an optimal learning environment. You'll reduce distraction and confusion, and free up classroom time for instruction.

The skills you will learn this week will help you give clear, confident directions that will keep your class working and keep you in charge.

There are five components for giving directions in Week Six:

> **HERE'S THE RESEARCH**
>
> Directions should be clear, unambiguous, and given in a manner that asserts the teacher's authority in the classroom (Emmer et al., 2002).

MONDAY Confidence

TUESDAY Rate and Volume

WEDNESDAY Steps

THURSDAY Triggers

FRIDAY Visual Cues

WEEK 1
WEEK 2
WEEK 3
WEEK 4
WEEK 5
WEEK 6
WEEK 7
WEEK 8

Confidence

When giving directions to students, look confident. Students know when a teacher is confident, prepared, and ready to teach, but also when they are unsure, doubtful, or hesitant. Having a confident teacher makes students feel more at ease in the classroom and can also affect learning outcomes.

HERE'S THE RESEARCH

Numerous studies have shown that student achievement is higher in classrooms with teachers who have more confidence (Ross, 1992; Goddard, 2000). Lack of confidence with classroom management has been identified as a major factor in teacher burnout (Browers, 2000).

Showing confidence helps you direct students with more authority. You must believe you are in charge of the classroom and expect your students to follow your directions. The key is in your physiology. Think like an actor—use your body and voice appropriately when giving directions. If you act confident, you *will* be confident.

Skill: **Body Language**

Here's how to do it:

Use body language to show confidence. Try all four of these ideas today.

- Feet—Plant your feet firmly about shoulder width apart. Do not dance around; stand solidly in one place.

- Hands—Position your hands with your palms facing down toward the floor. Palms up can signal indecisiveness; palms down indicate firmness and confidence.

- Gaze—Maintain a steady gaze while giving directions. Make slow and steady eye contact with your students. People who are unsure often have a gaze that darts around the room, or looks down at the floor or off into the distance. (Review week three's lesson on maintaining eye contact.)

- Gestures—Make your gestures really big; even bigger than you may think they should be. Gestures should have a definite starting and ending place.

I recommend practicing in front of a mirror to get comfortable with how you hold your hands, plant your feet, move your eyes, and gesture. If possible, ask someone you trust to watch you practice. It may feel peculiar at first, but you'll be much more comfortable when you're actually in the classroom in front of your students.

Here's an idea for showing confidence from the word of business:

- **Power Poses**

  What do you do if you don't feel confident? Research from Harvard Business School professor Amy Cuddy suggests: fake it 'til you make it.

  Cuddy says that a "power pose" is a way to show confidence even when you don't feel it. Her research has shown that if you

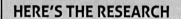

HERE'S THE RESEARCH

Using a Power Pose will help your tolerance for risk improve, and you will feel more powerful and actually be more powerful (Carney, Cuddy, and Yap, 2010).

stand in a power pose for one to two minutes, good things happen to you physically, physiologically, and behaviorally.

To do a power pose, stand like Superman or Wonder Woman—feet planted as wide as your shoulders, hands on hips, face determined, confident, and staring into the distance. That's it! Hold that pose for a minute or two, and your testosterone will go up and your cortisol, which is the chemical associated with stress, will go down. Sound too good to be true? Try it.

Rate and Volume

Speaking loudly enough for a student in any part of the classroom to hear the directions is important. But your rate of speaking, especially when giving directions, is equally important. Many teachers speak too fast when giving directions. The most effective speakers talk at a well-modulated rate of speech that is easy to understand. When teaching and giving directions, your rate of speech should be appropriate for the content that is being taught, the age of the students, and the space in which you are teaching.

Think about the population of students in your classroom. You might have students who have issues understanding you when you speak. For example, ESL (English as a Second Language) students will benefit from a slower pace of speech.

You might have students in your classroom with speech and language processing difficulties, or students with hearing loss.

To be most effective with all your students, make sure your volume and rate of speech helps you be understood. Today when giving directions, speak more slowly than usual and increase your voice volume.

HERE'S THE RESEARCH

Second language acquisition is greatly helped by the teacher slowing down his/her rate of speech when teaching (Zhao, 1997).

In one study, students with mild to severe hearing loss reported having more difficulty comprehending rapid speech and words that do not come up regularly in conversation (Kirk et al., 1997).

Research has indicated that children with ADHD may have impaired working memory, so a slower voice rate may help them comprehend the lesson (Martinussen, 2006).

Skill: Slow Down and Speak Up!

Here's how to do it:

Slow Down

In general, when giving directions, speak much slower than you feel you need to.

Taking into account our bilingual population, plus students with receptive language difficulties and hearing issues, you should stay far below the 200 words per minute threshold when giving directions. Try to pace your speech in the range of 130 to 150 words per minute.

HERE'S THE RESEARCH

Comprehension is compromised starting at approximately 200 words per minute for native speakers in conversation (Griffiths, 1990).

Be aware of your speech rate and consciously choose to say your words slower. Think of the pace of the words of the song "Twinkle, Twinkle, Little Star," and match your directions to that pace.

SPEECH RATE

To get an idea of your rate of speech, go to a website such as www.speechinminutes.com to calculate your rate of speech. Or you can copy your entire speech text into a website such as www.debatrix.com/en/training-coaching/speech-calculator-how-long-does-yours-take to calculate how long the speech will take at the rate you would like to speak.

Speak Up

- Make sure the volume of your voice is appropriate for the activity, the age and size of the group you are teaching to, and the space in which you are teaching. You don't want to be in a small classroom and sound like you are shouting. Feel free to vary the volume of your voice, as long as you are certain that you are loud enough for every child to easily hear and understand your directions. Ask a trusted colleague to sit in the very back of your classroom and give honest feedback to you on the volume of your voice.

- Try a sound system if you aren't loud enough for the size of your room. A built-in speaker system is ideal, but few classrooms have them. Portable speaker systems work and are not expensive.

Steps

It's easy to create classroom management problems with a few poorly thought-out directions. "Stand up and find partners. No wait, get into groups of five. Wait, go back, you will need your pencils and books for this . . ." Sounds like pandemonium about to break out!

Today, think your activities through first before you utter a word to help your students better follow your directions.

Skill: First, Next, Last

Here's how to do it:

1 Choose a task that you will do today that in your classroom for which you will need to give directions: for example, asking students to move from sitting at their desks to standing in small groups.

2 Now, think everything through. Write down each of the steps needed to give complete directions, including these components:

    a. What comes first, next, and last in the sequence of directions?

    b. Passing out resources
- How are you going to pass them out?
- Are you going to have students pick up papers as they walk into the room?
- Are you going to have a student helper pass out papers?
- Will you be using one volunteer from each group to come to your desk to get resources?

    c. Group considerations
- When do they get into groups?
- How many students in each group?
- Are the groups created by student choice, teacher choice, or in some other way?

- Where will the groups gather once they are created?
- Will you have them standing or sitting?
- Will they need to bring chairs with them to sit in?

d. Breaks
- Will they need a break before the lesson is over?
- Do you have one or two ideas that you could use to give them a break?

e. Will they need to give or receive feedback before the end of the lesson?

3 Test your directions by following them yourself before the students arrive. You'll quickly learn if you've gotten all the steps in the right order.

When you give your directions to the class for the chosen task today, follow your written notes. Use this approach for all your directions and within a few weeks, you won't need to write down the steps—you'll be giving clearer directions every time!

Triggers

Scene 1:

A teacher of a high school class says, "For this next activity, you will need partners . . ." And she has already lost them as students immediately begin to negotiate the social hierarchy of who will be partners with whom.

Scene 2:

The first grade teacher says, "Good job on the small shapes on this side of the room; now we will be moving over to the large shapes over here . . ." And he has already lost them as 28 first graders start racing toward the large shapes on the other side of the room.

Scene 3:

The middle school teacher says, "Today we will be going to the science lab . . ." And she has already lost them as 32 eighth graders suddenly push their chairs out, stand up, and head out the door.

In addition to giving clear directions, you need to have a process to give directions that keep students in place until you have completed giving directions, and also provides a signal for when it's time to start moving—*after* the directions have been given. I recommend a technique called "Four-Part Directions" from Rich Allen's book *High Impact Teaching Strategies in the 'XYZ' Era of Education* (2010, pp. 42-58).

Skill: **Four-Part Directions**

Here's how to do it:

Choose a specific activity you will be doing today that requires directions. It's best if it involves the students moving around the room in some way.

1 Start your directions by stating a time frame when the directions will be done and the students will start moving. The phrase you say to start your four-part directions is "In ten seconds . . ."

2 The second part of the directions is setting the trigger—the word you'll say to release the students to move. The trigger word is "Go." After you give the time frame, you say, "When I say 'go' . . ."

3 The third part, after you give the time frame and the trigger, is when you give the actual directions. Say the directions the way you normally would; for example: "Please stand and find a partner."

4 Now that the directions have been given, you release the trigger by saying the trigger word "Go!"

The entire sequence sounds like this:

"In ten seconds, when I say 'go,' please stand and find a partner. Go!"

TRIGGER WORDS

It can be fun to add novelty by giving a fun or random trigger word, such as "In ten seconds, when I say 'shoe horn' . . ."

Add a hand motion to further emphasize the directions: put your hands out in front of you, palms down, and hold them in that position as you say, "In ten seconds, when I say go, I want to you stand and find a partner." At the same time as you say the word "Go," push both hands down, like you are pushing two giant buttons that are in front of you.

Every time you give a direction, the last word that comes out of your mouth should be an action word. Don't say "Kids, when you're ready, get up and get your books, then sit back down, okay?" Try to end with an action word: "Kids, when I say 'go,' stand up, get your books, and sit back down—Go!"

Visual Cues

Spoken directions go more smoothly when visual cues are attached. Teachers of English as a Second Language know this—non-English speaking students force you to show direction visually. For students with a limited English vocabulary, directions such as "clockwise," "counter-clockwise," "left," "right," "forward," "backward," and "turn to your neighbor" may not be effective.

In addition to vocabulary, a common source of confusion is simple perspective. If you are facing the students and say "raise this hand" while raising your own right hand, students must interpret what they think you want them to do. Do you want them to mirror you and raise their left hands, since you are facing them? Or should they mentally rotate that hand in their minds and raise their right hand, which will look like the opposite hand since they are facing you?

Adding visual cues to your spoken directions will help everyone know exactly what you mean.

Skill: Anchors and Modeling

Here's how to do it:

Today, try both of these ways to add visual cues: using visual anchors for your directions and visually modeling the direction.

- **Visual anchors**
  Add something visual in the room to clarify your directions. For example, don't say, "Turn to the right." Find something on that side of the room, perhaps the door, and direct the students to "Turn toward the door side of the room." Instead of saying, "Raise this hand," find something as a visual anchor on that side of the room and tell the students to "Raise your window-side hand."

- **Visual modeling**
  Use gestures as you give the direction. For example, instead of saying, "Move

clockwise," make a big gesture with your hand in the direction you want the students to move, and say, "Move in this direction." (Besides, clockwise is becoming an outdated concept in our digital world!)

Week 7: Communicating

There is a passage in *Alice's Adventures in Wonderland* by Lewis Carroll that sums up the importance of clear communication:

> "Then you should say what you mean," the March Hare went on.
>
> "I do," Alice hastily replied; "at least—at least I mean what I say— that's the same thing, you know."
>
> "Not the same thing a bit!" said the Hatter. "You might just as well say that 'I see what I eat' is the same thing as 'I eat what I see'!"

As teachers, spoken communication is how we do our jobs. What we say can hurt or heal, encourage a spirit or crush motivation. Our words can get groups of students moving and actively engaged in activity; they can invite an individual student to be self-reflective and introspective. Taking charge of how you communicate can add to a well-run classroom when done correctly and create havoc when done poorly.

Learning to communicate appropriately with students is an essential classroom management skill. This week's skills will help you be a more effective communicator.

There are five components for communicating in Week Seven:

MONDAY Pausing

TUESDAY Non-words

WEDNESDAY Clarity

THURSDAY Encouragment

FRIDAY No Multitasking

WEEK 1
WEEK 2
WEEK 3
WEEK 4
WEEK 5
WEEK 6
WEEK 7
WEEK 8

WEEK 7
Pausing

L ast week, you learned how to slow down your rate of speech so students could clearly understand you in the classroom. Today, we'll refine that skill by taking a pause now and then to allow students to improve their comprehension.

All students need time to consciously and unconsciously process what they are hearing and seeing.

When you pause in your oral communication, you'll see lots of benefits:

- Responses by students will become longer and more accurate.

- Fewer students will respond, "I don't know."

- More students will give appropriate answers.

- Your students' test scores are likely to improve.

Don't be afraid to take a pause!

HERE'S THE RESEARCH

Some students, such as those with ADHD, may take a little longer to process information (Martinussen, 2006).

Most teachers wait only one second before calling on a student to answer (Row, 1986).

Waiting a few extra seconds can improve the length and correctness of the students' responses, and fewer students will give an "I don't know" or "no" answer. Students' scores on academic achievement tests have been found to increase using this pausing technique (Stahl, 1990; 1994).

Skill: Hit the Pause Button

Here's how to do it:

Today, try pausing in at least one of the following situations:

- **When presenting information-rich visuals**
  When a new visual is shown, especially a visual that has a lot of information

on it, pause for a few extra seconds while you are looking at the visual, giving students time to digest the information presented.

During a lecture

Pause occasionally during your lecture and wait a few seconds without saying anything, giving the students time to write notes. If they are writing, they are not fully listening to what you are saying.

HERE'S THE RESEARCH

Although taking notes during a lecture can aid in recall and raise test scores later, note taking may interfere with immediate retention of information during the lecture (Faber et al., 2000).

When calling on students to respond

Wait at least three to five seconds to call on students to respond to a question or a class discussion prompt, even if some hands are up. You're likely to see more hands go up in that short interval.

Before giving important information

When you are giving out important information, such as the date of a test or announcing grades, pause. Wait a breath before telling the news. It will add drama, and everyone will be sure to listen more carefully.

When reading aloud

Wait a breath or two at a critical moment in the story, to make the reading more dramatic. It may sound like a very long pause to you, but to the audience it will sound just right.

Non-words

WEEK 7

Today you'll learn to clean up your speech by avoiding or eliminating distracting speech sounds in your spontaneous speech. Minor vocal tics can be lessened and even eliminated when you work on them.

About half the speech sounds we make are non-words, or disfluencies. There are three types of disfluencies: filled pauses (with "um," "uh," or another non-word), repeated words ("Please take a pen—a pen—a pen with you to your group"), and sentence restarts (Please take a pen—I mean pen—I mean, Please take a pencil with you to your group"). Disfluencies can convey the message that the speaker is not confident and is unsure of what to say next.

HERE'S THE RESEARCH

The biggest disfluency is "um," which is second only to "the" as the most used word in conversation (Bates, Masling, and Kintsch, 1978).

The frequency of "ums" does not seem to increase with anxiety (Mahl, 1987), nor are there more "ums" in a speech by someone not experienced in speaking about the topic (Schachter et al., 1991). "Ums" do increase when the speaker is using large, multisyllabic vocabulary (Schachter et al., 1991), thinking about several complex options at once (Schachter et al., 1991), or if the topic is more abstract (Lay and Paivio, 1969).

But take heart! Just paying attention and trying to speak with fewer disfluencies has been shown to be an effective tool for helping to eliminate them in spontaneous speech (Shriberg, 2005).

Today's skill to help you lose the non-words will not be practiced in the classroom, but maybe in the teacher's room with a colleague. It's a quick game called "My First Car."

Skill: My First Car

Here's how to do it:

1 Find a friend. Another teacher who wants to clear out the "ums" would be a perfect partner for this game.

2 Have your partner listen to you as you tell the story of your first car—how you bought it, what color and make it was, where you were living when you got it, and so on. As soon as you say your first "uh" or "um," your partner stops you.

3 Now it's your partner's turn to start giving you his/her first car story. When you hear your partner's first "um," switch again!

4 Five minutes of this game is enough for both of you to focus on speaking smoothly without the verbal tics.

5 If you want to play this game again, add repetitive phrases that you or your partner may use without thinking. (Do you say "like," or "okay" more than you should? Maybe your favorite phrase is "so to speak.") Repetitive phrases are another kind of verbal tic that can be not only annoying to listeners but disruptive to a class. Students often giggle or act out when they hear the same phrase used by the teacher over and over again.

FILL THE GAP WITH SILENCE
Instead of using "uh," "um," or a repetitive phrase, fill the gap in your thinking with silence, not sound. Remember yesterday's skill—and take a pause.

Clarity

When getting students' attention, starting a lesson, passing out resources, or whenever you are talking to students, it is important to get to the point right away. Be clear about what you need from your students.

This is one of our rules for adults in the school where I am principal. "Ask for what you need" is what all our new teachers hear the first time they step into the building. It means: don't be afraid to ask questions, don't hesitate to get advice and mentoring, and never wait to ask for resources. It also means: be clear in your communication with colleagues, students, and parents. And it also means: if something is bothering you, don't complain in the teacher's lounge. Bring it up at a meeting or with the person with whom you have an issue.

In the classroom, "Ask for what you need" means: be clear in your communication with students. Make sure your communication doesn't show favoritism, is unambiguous, and demonstrates your expectations.

Today, you are going to practice being clear and direct with your students in all facets of your spoken communication.

Skill: Ask for What You Need

Here's how to do it:

Try either or both of these ideas today when you want to get attention or start your lesson. Both of them make it clear to the students exactly what you need.

- **To get students' attention:**

Tell the whole class that you want their attention. Say in a calm voice, "Look up at me and stop talking now." This kind of language lets students know exactly what you are looking for, and reinforces the student behaviors that are needed for learning.

Too often, teachers try to get students' attention by praising other students who are acting appropriately. If you say, "I like the way Greg is listening and ready to learn," that does not let students know what you want. You could embarrass Greg, and it could make other students resentful of him. The statement is ambiguous, and it takes the students' attention away from the teacher while everyone checks out Greg to see what he is doing.

Just tell them exactly what you want them to do.

● To start the lesson:

Keep communication brief and to the point. "Stop talking now and give me your full attention so we may start the lesson." Then wait until you get 100 percent of all the students' attention.

Do *not* begin your lesson this way: "Students, I have worked very hard on this lesson and I am not going to start until everyone of you is sitting on your bottoms, hands in your laps, and looking up at me. Talking while I'm talking is disrespectful and just not nice. I'm sure your mother and father have raised you better than that. Is that clear?"

Just get to the point and ask for what you need!

Encouragement

Encouragement improves classroom management and decreases off-task, disruptive, and anti-social behavior. But what do we encourage, and what words do we say to have the most impact? The answer is to be found in research on a concept called "mindsets."

Researcher Carol Dweck has identified two types of mindset: the fixed mindset and the growth mindset (2008). People with a fixed mindset believe that their intelligence is set from birth and

HERE'S THE RESEARCH

A study done in 2008 by the US Department of Education showed that students who believed that their math ability was something they were born with and couldn't develop regardless of how much effort they put into learning the material had significantly less persistence on complex tasks than those who believed that they could improve through effort.

they're not going to change that very much throughout their lives. But with a growth mindset, people believe their abilities can change over time.

Focusing on praising effort rather than achievement can nurture a growth mindset in your students. When you praise effort by saying, "You did really well on that math test. You must have studied hard!" you encourage students to persist in the task. Students with a growth mindset ask questions in class and get excited by difficult problems, because they see these as opportunities to grow.

Now that you have made your classroom a risk-free zone for participation, students will respond when you encourage them to do more and praise them for the effort they have put forth.

HERE'S THE RESEARCH

In several studies, when the instructor encouraged answers and gave feedback immediately to students, the amount of participation increased and had a positive effect on learning (Gorhman, 1988; Menzel, 1999).

Skill: Praise the Effort

Here's how to do it:

Today, try praising students for the effort they put into an assignment, not the skill or ability they may possess.

For example, say, "You must have put in a great deal of effort to get that grade. I'm proud of the effort you put into this assignment!" rather than, "You got a good grade on that last math test! You were just born to do this advanced math, weren't you?"

Here are more ideas to give effective encouragement that you can try in the upcoming days and weeks. The situations to use them are bound to arise in your classroom.

- ### Use Words and Body Language
  When a student is answering a question, volunteering, or trying his/her best at a difficult task, be encouraging in your words and body language. Lean forward slightly toward the student and encourage him/her with an occasional "Oh, I see," and "Yes, you're on the right track." Give eye contact, a slight head nod, and a smile.

- ### Avoid "Comfort Talks"
  If you have a student who is not getting it, don't try to comfort the student by saying things like "Bless your heart," "Plenty of people have trouble with this," "You have other strengths," or "Not everyone is cut out to pursue a career in this field."

> **HERE'S THE RESEARCH**
>
> "Comfort" comments have been shown to be a strong de-motivator because they lower the student's expectations of him/herself (Rattan et al., 2012). They change a student's internal picture of him/herself as a learner, and the student begins to predict that he/she will do poorly. Students' predictions of their own success are a strong indicator of their actual achievement (Yamagata et al., 2012).

- ### Help Students Encourage Themselves
  The act of looking for successful outcomes will encourage students to recognize

when they happen. Try these ideas:

a. Have students write a journal entry at the end of every day about something they did in school in which they experienced success. The successful event can be small or large. Make sure they describe the effort they put forth to make this success possible.

b. Have students write a note to their parents about a recent success they have had in class.

c. Have students chart their own progress in a personal data folder. For example, students can write their pretest scores and then chart the scores of their formative assessments. Charting your own growth is a great motivator.

WEEK 7

No Multitasking

Have you ever tried to talk at the same time you're writing on the board? It's hard to do, but teachers try because they don't want to stop teaching and want to keep their students engaged.

Human beings don't multitask well, despite what we may think. It's like a bottleneck in the brain, where only one decision-making task can be processed at a time. This is why we shouldn't try to write on the board while carrying on a conversation with the class.

Today, separate writing on the board from talking to the class.

HERE'S THE RESEARCH

When we try to do two tasks at once, one of them must wait until the other is completed (Dux, 2006).

Skill: Writing, Then Talking

Here's how to do it:

1 Write on the board without speaking to the class. Don't write for more than ten seconds at a time.

2 When the content has been written, then turn and continue teaching.

Try these alternatives to trying to write and speak at the same time:

* Have a student act as scribe as you talk, so that you can continue to monitor the class.

* Write the information on the board before the students enter the classroom.

* Write the information on a flip chart before class so you can point to

the topics as they come up when you are speaking.

- Use an overhead projector to display information.

- Use a document camera that automatically projects what is under the lens.

- Use an interactive whiteboard to have a student act as scribe, or have pre-written notes that you can display on the whiteboard.

Week 8: Transitioning

In school, there are countless transitions that occur every day. Class begins, class ends. The class breaks into groups. The class returns from groups. You take a break. You get started again after the break. Every transition is an opportunity for some students in your class to lose focus and create discipline issues.

HERE'S THE RESEARCH

Classroom routines affect students' behavior positively, as well as their academic achievement (Cheney, 1989; Vallecorsa, deBettencourt, and Zigmond, 2000).

To take charge of all transitions, here's a strategy that works: create a routine for each transition. When you have routines for the activities that happen daily, you create a predictable environment in the classroom that students can count on. You are handling the situation, often without having to say a word.

Start by thinking about the activities that occur every day, such as hanging up coats, using the restroom, sharpening pencils, and getting supplies, and create routines for each. Other routines can focus on activities related to classroom instruction, such getting students' attention and reviewing information. Write down step-by-step directions you use for each of these daily activities. Think them through and create routines for each. Then make sure that you teach them to your students so everyone knows the expectations.

This week, you will learn routines for some common transitions in the classroom, including starting the lesson and stopping the lesson, grouping students successfully, and moving from one activity to another.

There are five components for transitioning in Week Eight:

MONDAY Starting   **THURSDAY** Groups

TUESDAY Stopping   **FRIDAY** Transition Control

WEDNESDAY Transition Directions

Starting

When students begin the day with a routine, they get their minds and bodies ready to learn.

Today, you'll use one of these two starting routines—one is high-energy and the other is quieter and less active. Both involve music, based on significant

HERE'S THE RESEARCH

One of the characteristics identified in all expert teachers was the use of well-practiced routines (Leinhardt and Greeno, 1986).

research on its effect on the brain's dopamine production. Choose one of the routines to try today, depending on your style, your comfort zone, and your class needs. Try the other one another day to see how your class responds to a different energy level.

Skill: **Starting Routine**

Here's how to do it:

Starting routine—high energy option:
A high-energy start to the day will help increase your students' dopamine levels.

1 When class is about to begin, play a fast-paced, high-energy song.

2 The students stand up and clap in time with the music.

3 After a few bars of music, say, "faster!" and clap faster than the beat, ignoring the beat of the music. After a few more bars, say, "faster!" again, and clap as fast as you can.

4 After everyone has been clapping quickly for a few seconds, the students hold one hand up over their heads and one hand down towards the ground.

5 The students bring their hands together with a clap while shouting, "Whoa!"

6 On that clap, the teacher stops the music, the students immediately sit down, and you are ready to start.

> **HERE'S THE RESEARCH**
>
> Music has been found to help with the transmission of dopamine throughout the brain (Sutoo and Akiyama, 2004).

Starting routine—lower energy option:

1 When class is about to start, begin playing a high-energy song.

2 Announce that class will be starting in one minute.

3 After approximately one minute (usually after the chorus of the song), stop the music. It is important to stop the music precisely at the same place every time so this becomes a routine. Begin to speak immediately after the music stops.

> **HERE'S THE RESEARCH**
>
> Listening to music can release dopamine into our systems (Salimpoor et al., 2011).

Here's another starting routine that gets everyone clapping and happy.

• The Power of Seven

1 Sit down in front of the class, visible to all the students. If the students are sitting on the floor, you should sit in a chair. If they are sitting at desks, you should sit on the edge of your desk or on a tall stool.

2 Tell students you are going to teach them three sets of movements. Each set is made up of seven movements. You model the movement first, and then say, "one-two-ready-go" and the students will repeat the pattern.

3 First pattern: Hit your lap with both of your hands seven times in row. Then say, "one-two-ready-go," and the students do the movements with you.

4 Second pattern: Hit your lap, then clap, then lap, clap, lap, clap, lap. Then say, "one-two-ready-go," and the students repeat the movements with you.

5 Do the first and second set of movements again, and then say, "one-two-ready-go," and the students repeat the first two sets of movements.

6 Third pattern: lap, clap, hands in the air next to your head, clap, lap, clap, hands in the air next to your head. Then say, "one-two-ready-go," and the students do the third set of movements with you.

7 Model all three sets of movements in a row, slowly, without stopping. Then say, "One-two-ready-go," and slowly do all three sets of movements with the students.

8 You will need to practice the routine a few times before everyone has it correctly. Once they know it, you can use it as a starting routine.

WEEK 7

Stopping

In school, a bell often signals the end of class. But whether or not your school uses bells, you will create a more predictable environment if you develop some stopping routines to follow. Don't be that teacher who is still shouting out directions and assignments as the students file out the door! Do your stopping routine one minute or two before the end of class.

Skill: Stopping Routine

Here's how to do it:

Today, use at least one of the three stopping routines described below:

* In, Out, Down
* Count Down
* Yellow Light

Experiment with all three and soon you'll discover which work best with your students.

• In, Out, Down

This is a great routine to stop activities when students are standing. It helps them stop and refocus for the next activity.

1 Make sure students are standing next to their chairs.

2 Tell students, "Take a deep breath in, hold it, and let it out."

3 Then say, "Take another deep breath in, hold it, and as you let it out, slowly sit down."

• Count Down

Cognitively difficult tasks, such as analysis or synthesis of information, require more attention on the students' part. When the teacher tries to stop those kinds of tasks without any warning, the part of the student's brain that is engaged in conversation may not be able to switch focus. A verbal Count Down by the teacher to let the students know that they need to begin to disengage from their conversation helps students stop.

1 Put students into groups or pairs.

2 Give students a discussion prompt.

3 Walk around the room to monitor conversations.

4 With two minutes left for discussion time, announce to the class: "You have about two minutes left."

5 At the one-minute mark, announce to the students "One minute left." In one minute, call time. Students will be able to stop comfortably.

6 Reinforce your Count Down with gestures. Hold up two fingers as you announce, "About two minutes left," then hold up one finger at "One minute left." Even better, have students look up and engage with you by holding up two fingers and announcing, "About this many minutes left." This makes it necessary for them to look up and see how many minutes you are indicating with your fingers.

COUNT DOWN GROUP DISCUSSIONS

For a fast way to stop group discussions, start counting down out loudly from five, while holding the corresponding number of fingers up. Say, "I need your attention in five . . . four . . . three . . . two . . . one . . . " and then you have it!

When closing out a class question-and-answer session, you can use Count Down to help students know how many more responses you will be taking before the end of a discussion. Say, "Before we move on, I'll take two more responses." Take two more, then that's it!

Yellow Light

When you give students permission to begin a discussion, you're giving them a "green light" to go ahead and start interacting. Then without warning, teachers give a "red light" and stop the conversation when it's time to begin asking the class questions. They need "yellow lights" between the green light ("Go ahead and begin to discuss") and the red light ("Give me three causes for the Great Depression"). When the time for discussion is near the end, use the four-step Yellow Light routine:

1 Tell them that the discussion time is drawing to a close by giving them a Count Down: "You have fifteen seconds left . . ."

2 Say, "Please find a place to pause that conversation."

3 Direct your students to give their partners an acknowledgment. Say "Give your partner a high-five and say 'thank you very much!'"

4 Announce, "Please turn your attention back to me."

From there, you continue on with the rest of the lesson. Using a yellow light routine allows students to wrap up the conversation and refocus on you.

Transition Directions

Imagine a teacher of an eighth grade science class trying to transition a class from the classroom to the science lab stations like this:

"Good morning students! We are going to the science lab today. When we get into the lab, please get into your lab groups. If you forgot who is in your lab group, check the list in the back of the room by the chemical cabinet. When you get to your lab station, I need one person to get about 18 inches of rubber tubing. Another person needs to get an Erlenmeyer flask—remember, it is wide at the bottom and skinny at the top. We have only three rules—One, Safety, Two, Safety, and Three, Safety, so we need another lab partner to go to the ultraviolet cabinet and get the safety goggles. I also need someone to light the Bunsen burner—remember, no more than one thumb length high—remember what happened to Bill last month. If you have only three people in your group today, then the person who got the rubber tubing can also light the Bunsen burner. Once that is all set, reach into the right hand side of your lab station and get your textbooks out. On page 147 is a picture of a volcano that has a little something to do with our experiment today."

This transition is a guaranteed disaster. The typical student will remember that they are going to the science lab today (the first thing said) and that what they are doing has something to do with a volcano (the last thing said). The directions in between are pretty fuzzy.

Don't make this kind of mistake! Give only one direction at a time. It will drastically reduce, or even eliminate, any off-task behaviors during the transition. This idea comes from Rich Allen's book *High Impact Teaching in the 'XYZ' Era of Education* (2010, p. 42-58). Allen gave us "Four-Part Directions" in Week Six and now helps us give more complicated directions for a transition, one at a time.

Skill: One Direction at a Time

Here's how to do it:

1 Think through all of the steps in the transition before you start giving directions to the students.

2 Give the students the first direction.

3 Wait until the first task is completed before giving the next direction. This is challenging to teachers, because they are always thinking ahead, monitoring the classroom, checking the clock, etc. Waiting for students to complete one step in a direction may seem like wasting time, but it will be quicker in the end, because there will be less confusion and less need to repeat directions.

The transition from classroom to science lab, using one direction at a time, might now sound like this:

1 "Good morning students! We are going to the science lab today. So, make sure your hands are free, and please stand up! (Wait for 100 percent of the class to be standing.)

2 "Raise your hand if you need a reminder who is in your lab group." (If there are no hands raised, continue.)

3 "Now, take a deep breath in, and now, let it out."

4 "Keep breathing normally—the next time I ask you to take a breath, I want you to hold it until we get to your lab stations. What questions may I answer?" (If there are no questions, continue).

5 "Take a deep breath—hold it—now don't let it out until we get to your lab stations."

6 Continue the rest of the directions in a similar manner. Give one direction, wait until it is complete, and then give the next small step in the sequence.

HOLD YOUR BREATH AND MOVE

I often use the "hold your breath and move" idea. There is usually plenty of cheating going on, with students sneaking breaths, but it doesn't matter—they aren't talking while they are moving!

Groups

Groups give students a chance to interact, share ideas, and test hypotheses in a lower-risk environment. But getting students into groups can be fraught with danger if not managed well. Putting students into groups without any facilitation by the teacher can result in groups of different sizes, students being excluded from groups, and cliques forming in the classroom.

These methods work well to get students into groups or pairs. You and your students might even have some fun along the way!

Skill: Getting into Groups

Here's how to do it:
Try at least one of these ways to group or pair your students today.

Groups:
- Students count off by the number of groups you need, and then form groups of those numbers.
- Hand out playing cards at random. All of the students with kings find each other and go in one group, all the students with aces form another group, etc.
- Find some small, funny items like refrigerator magnets and buy at least four each of several different designs. Have enough magnets for the number of students in your class. Put the magnets in a bag, and let students each pull out one. Each group is formed with all the students who have picked the same magnet.

Pairs:
- Create pairs of notecards: one card has a joke, the other card has the punch line. Laminate the cards for a set you can use many times.

Students find each other to pair up.

- Use content-specific notecards to form pairs. For example, write synonyms on cards for partners to find: one card says "cold" and the partner card says "freezing"; or two antonyms: one card says "good" the partner card says "evil." In a chemistry class: one card says "H_2O," and the partner card says "water."

- Put sets of two objects into a bag and have each student draw one object from the bag. Pairs are formed with the partner who has the matching object. You can use pairs of candies (two Jolly Ranchers, two Kit Kat bars, two green M&Ms, etc.), paint samples from the local hardware store (two eggshell white squares, two burnt ochre, etc.), two unsharpened colored pencils (two orange pencils, two red pencils, etc.). This method is limited only by your imagination and budget!

GROUPING IDEAS

Students often work well with their friends, but they might be tempted to chat and waste time with students they know well. Sometimes you'll want to randomly group students.

Usually, you'll want to have all groups complete a task at about the same time. Make groups the same size. A group with four students will usually be finished sooner than a group with six members.

Make it clear with your class that any student may be in a group with any other student. No favoritism and no cliques allowed!

Transition Control

WEEK 8

F

Throughout the school day, you're shifting from one activity to another. Although keeping the class active can keep students interested, there are many opportunities for chaos during transitions.

Teachers need to be in control of transitions from one activity to another. Following the five steps of the transition cascade will lead to flawless activity shifts. Just like a cascade of water, each step in the transition cascade flows directly into the other.

The transition cascade has five steps:

1 Get students' attention

2 Shift students' focus to the teacher

3 End the activity

4 Give directions for the next activity

5 Start new activity

Making a smooth transition from one activity to another offers the opportunity to practice a number of the skills you have learned over the last eight weeks. Select skills that have worked well for your class, or experiment with ones you haven't tried yet.

Skill: **Transition Cascade**

Here's how to do it:

1 **Get students' attention**

Some students may need help getting their attention away from the task in which they are engaged. Use ideas from Week One: Getting Attention, such as **Novel Sounds, Cross Clap**, or **Lap-Clap-Snap**. Make sure you're in your teaching spot when you get the students' attention so they are already cued that you are now in charge.

2 Shift students' focus to the teacher

After you have the students' attention, they need to shift their attention to you.

Use skills from previous weeks, including **Making Eye Contact** or **Sit and Shhh!** Sometimes just standing next to a student who is having difficulty shifting focus can work wonders.

3 End the activity

Try some of the ideas from Week Eight: Stopping, such as **In, Out, Down** or **Yellow Light**. When students are familiar with the classroom stopping routines, they'll understand that when you do one of these, the activity is over.

4 Give directions for the next activity

Give clear, concise directions with confidence, using skills from Week Six: Giving Directions, such as **Four-Part Directions**, **First, Next, Last**, and **Anchors and Modeling**.

5 Start new activity

Start a new activity *together*. It is frustrating when a lesson begins and has to stop because someone isn't in the right place or doesn't understand the directions. To help ensure a collective start to the next activity, try using ideas from Week Eight: Starting, such as the high- or low-energy **Starting Routines**. This could be the perfect time for a short break, so try one from Week Two: Keeping Attention. Even a very short break can refresh the group and help your students be ready to start on their next learning adventure with you!

Final Thoughts
A Lesson from the Termites

Congratulations! You have learned at least forty skills that will put you well on your way to mastering management of your classroom.

Some of the skills will take longer to incorporate into daily use than others. Take note of these and circle back to them. Use the next few weeks to build your level of comfort with these skills or to try some of the optional skills in the chapters. Don't focus on too many new skills at once.

Take a lesson from the termites . . .

Research at the University of Colorado (Moellenberg, 2003) showed that in the United States, termites do more damage every year to homes than fires. Bite by bite, those little guys are more devastating than an inferno.

The message of the termites is clear. If you want to make real change, settle in for the long haul. Take little nibbles every lesson, every hour, every day of teaching. Hundreds and thousands of little bites, and before long, you will have made huge changes.

Heath and Heath (2007) call this "Shrinking the Change." I think about this concept when I have a big job to do, like cleaning the basement. That job is so overwhelming I don't even want to get started. But if I tell myself I will work for only five minutes right now, then I will start the job, maybe by picking up any magazines lying around. Once that is done, invariably I am motivated to do another small step. That leads to another and another, until the job is complete.

So act like a termite and bite off these skills one at a time. Before you know it, you and your students will have incorporated the ones that really work in your classroom, and everyone will be more productive.

Best of luck to you as you continue to master classroom management!

Acknowledgments

First and foremost, I must acknowledge the originality and brilliance of Dr. Rich Allen. Dr. Allen taught me the great value of learning observable, discrete skills to enhance my professional practice. Thanks, Rich!

I must pay homage to Bobbi DePorter and the staff at Quantum Learning Network. They all epitomize the growth mindset, and are the gold standard by which I measure my efforts. I would also like to thank the decade of students at Oakland University in Rochester, Michigan, whose willingness to push their abilities and work outside their comfort zone made it possible for me to create these skills in my apprenticeship of practice in the trenches with all of you and the thousands of presentations in which I was privileged to be a part. I must also thank the staff at Erie Elementary School, Clinton Township, Michigan, from whom I have learned so much.

Thanks to readers of early drafts of this book, including Marcy Walsh, Robert Egan, and Brent Vasicek. Your comments were right on, and your enthusiasm was humbling. I thank my brothers and sisters, Bob, Dan, Sandy, Trudy, Dorie, Deb, Steve, Tricia, and Charles, for their support and encouragement my entire life.

Most of all, I am so grateful to my wife and daughters for understanding when Dad came home late, again, because he was working on this book. Thanks for understanding and supporting me.

Bibliography

Adams, Rebecca, Paul Finn, Elisabeth Moes, Kathleen Flannery, and Albert Rizzo. "Distractibility in Attention/Deficit/ Hyperactivity Disorder (ADHD): The Virtual Reality Classroom," *Child Neuropsychology: A Journal on Normal and Abnormal Development in Childhood and Adolescence* 15, no. 2 (2009): 120-35.

Aibali, Martha W., Miriam Bassok, Karen Olseth-Solomon, Sharon E. Syc, and Susan Goldin-Meadow. "Illuminating Mental Representations through Speech and Gesture." *Psychological Science* 19, no. 3 (1999): 327-33.

Allday, R. Allan, and Kerri Pakurar. "Effects of Teacher Greetings on Student On-task Behavior." *Journal of Communication* 19 no. 2, (2007): 157-62.

Allday, R. Allan, Miranda Bush, Nicole Ticknor, and Lindsay Walker. "Using Teacher Greetings to Increase Speed to Task Engagement." *Journal of Applied Behavior Analysis* 44, no. 2 (2011): 393-96.

Allen, Richard H. *Impact Teaching Strategies in the 'XYZ' Era of Education.* Boston: Allyn and Bacon, 2010.

Allen, Vernon L., and David A. Wilder. "Impact of Group Consensus and Social Support on Stimulus Meaning: Mediation of Conformity by Cognitive Restructuring." *Journal of Personality and Social Psychology* 39, no. 6 (1980): 1116-24.

Althoff, Sarah E., Kristen J. Linde, John D. Mason, Ninja M. Nagel, and Katie A. O'Reilly. "Learning Objectives: Posting and Communicating Daily Learning Objectives to Increase Student Achievement and Motivation." *ERIC Online Submission* (2007).

Anderson, John R. "A Spreading Activation Theory of Memory." Journal of Verbal Learning and Verbal Behavior 22, no. 3 (1983): 261-95.

Atwood, Virginia A., and William W. Wilen. "Wait Time and Effective Social Studies Instruction: What Can Research in Science Education Tell Us?" *Social Education* 55, no. 3 (1991): 179-81.

Bass, Joel L., Michael Corwin, David Gozal, Carol Moore, Hiroshi Nishida, Steven Parker, Alison Schonwald, Richard E. Wilker, Sabine Stehle, and T. Bernard Kinane. "The Effect of Chronic or Intermittent Hypoxia on Cognition in Childhood: A Review of the Evidence." *Pediatrics* 114, no. 3 (2004): 805-816.

Bates, Elizabeth, Mark Masling, and Walter Kintsch. "Recognition Memory for Aspects of Dialogue." *Journal of Experimental Psychology: Human Learning and Memory* 4, no. 3 (1978): 187.

Blackburn, Robert T., Glenn R. Pellino, Alice Boberg, and Colman O'Connell. "Are Instructional Improvement Programs Off Target?" *Current Issues in Higher Education* 2, no. 1 (1980): 32-48.

Blood, Anne J., and Robert J. Zatorre. "Intensely Pleasurable Responses to Music Correlate with Activity in Brain Regions Implicated in Reward and Emotion." *Proceedings of the National Academy of Sciences* 98, no. 20 (2001): 11818-823.

Bloom, Floyd E., M. F. Beal, and D. Kupfer, eds. *The Dana Guide to Brain Health: A Practical Family Reference from Medical Experts.* New York: Dana Press, 2002.

Bohn, Roger E., and James E. Short. *How Much Information?: 2009 Report on American Consumers.* University of California, San Diego, Global Information Industry Center, 2009.

Booth, James R., Lydia Wood, Dong Lu, James C. Houk, and Tali Bitan. "The Role of the Basal Ganglia and Cerebellum in Language Processing." *Brain Research* 1133, no. 1 (2007): 136-44.

Boushel, Robert, Henning Langberg, Simon Green, Dorthe Skovgaard, Jens Bülow, and Michael Kjær. "Blood Flow and Oxygenation in Peritendinous Tissue and Calf Muscle during Dynamic Exercise in Humans." *The Journal of Physiology* 524, no. 1 (2000): 305-13.

Bove, A. A., J. D. Dewey, and G. M. Tyce. "Increased Conjugated Dopamine in Plasma after Exercise Training." *The Journal of Laboratory and Clinical Medicine* 104, no. 1 (1984): 77-85.

Broaders, Sara C., Susan Wagner Cook, Zachary Mitchell, and Susan Goldin-Meadow. "Making Children Gesture Brings Out Implicit Knowledge and Leads to Learning." *Journal of Experimental Psychology General* 136, no.4 (2007): 539-50.

Brouwers, André, and Welko Tomic. "A Longitudinal Study of Teacher Burnout and Perceived Self-Efficacy in Classroom Management." *Teaching and Teacher Education* 16, no. 2 (2000): 239-53.

Bunce, Diane M., Elizabeth A. Flens, and Kelly Y. Neiles. "How Long Can Students Pay Attention in Class? A Study of Student Attention Decline Using Clickers." *Journal of Chemical Education* 87, no. 12 (2010): 1438-43.

Caldji, Christian, Beth Tannenbaum, Shakti Sharma, Darlene Francis, Paul M. Plotsky, and Michael J. Meaney. "Maternal Care during Infancy Regulates the Development of Neural Systems Mediating the Expression of Fearfulness in the Rat." *Proceedings of the National Academy of Sciences of the United States of America* 95, no. 9 (1998): 5335-40.

Carney, Dana R., Amy J. C. Cuddy, and Andy J. Yap. "Power Posing: Brief Nonverbal Displays Affect Neuroendocrine Levels and Risk Tolerance." *Psychological Science* 21, no. 10 (2010): 1363-68.

Caspi, Avner, Eran Chajut, and Kelly Saporta. "Participation in Class and in Online Discussions: Gender Differences." *Computers & Education* 50, no. 3 (2008): 718-24.

Chang, Hao-chieh. The Effect of News Teasers in Processing TV News. *Journal of Broadcasting & Electronic Media* 42, no. 3 (1998): 327-39.

Cheney, Christine O. "Preventive Discipline through Effective Classroom Management." *ERIC Digest* (April 1989): ERIC Number: ED304869

Chun, Marvin M., and Yuhong Jiang. "Contextual Cueing: Implicit Learning and Memory of Visual Context Guides Spatial Attention." *Cognitive Psychology* 36, no. 1 (1998): 28-71.

Courchesne, Eric, and Greg Allen. "Prediction and Preparation, Fundamental Functions of the Cerebellum." *Learning & Memory* 4, no. 1 (1997): 1-15.

Crestani, Fabio. "Application of Spreading Activation Techniques in Information Retrieval." *Artificial Intelligence Review* 11, no. 6 (1997): 453-82.

Crowder, Elaine. "Gestures at Work in Sense-Making Science Talk." *Journal of the Learning Sciences* 5, no. 3, (1996): 173-208.

Damon, William. "Peer Education: The Untapped Potential." *Journal of Applied Developmental Psychology* 5, no. 4, (1984): 331-43.

Damasio, A. R. *The Feeling of What Happens: Body and Emotion in the Making of Consciousness.* New York: Houghton Mifflin Harcourt, 1999.

Davis, R. H., and L. T. Alexander. "The Lecture Method," In *Guides for the Improvement of Instruction in Higher Education No. 5,* East Lansing, MI: Michigan State University, 1977.

Desimone, Robert, and John Duncan. "Neural Mechanisms of Selective Visual Attention." *Annual Review of Neuroscience* 18 (1995): 193-222.

Desmond, John E., John D. E. Gabrieli, Anthony D. Wagner, Bruce L. Ginier, and Gary H. Glover. "Lobular Patterns of Cerebellar Activation in Verbal Working-Memory and Finger-Tapping Tasks as Revealed by Functional MRI." *The Journal of Neuroscience* 17, no. 24 (1997): 9675-85.

Diamond, Marian, and Janet Hopson. *Magic Trees of the Mind: How to Nurture Your Child's Intelligence, Creativity, and Healthy Emotions from Birth through Adolescence.* New York: Plume Books, 1999.

Dillon, James T. "The Remedial Status of Student Questioning." *Journal of Curriculum Studies* 20, no. 3 (1988): 197-210.

DiMatteo, M. Robin, Ron D. Hays, and Louise M. Prince. "Relationship of Physicians' Nonverbal Communication Skill to Patient Satisfaction, Appointment Noncompliance, and Physician Workload." *Health Psychology* 5, no. 6 (1986): 581-94.

Dineen, John P., Hewitt B. Clark, and Todd R. Risley. "Peer Tutoring among Elementary Students: Educational Benefits to the Tutor." *Journal of Applied Behavior Analysis*, 10, no. 2 (1977): 231-38.

Dux, Paul E., Jason Ivanoff, Christopher L. Asplund, and Rene Marois. "Isolation of a Central Bottleneck of Information Processing with Time-Resolved fMRI." *Neuron* 52, no. 6 (2006): 1109-20.

Dweck, Carol. *Mindset: The New Psychology of Success.* New York: Random House, 2008.

Ebbinghaus, Hermann. *On Memory: A Contribution to Experimental Psychology.* New York: Teachers College, 1913.

Ellis, B. H., P. A. Fisher, and S. Zaharie. "Predictors of Disruptive Behavior, Developmental Delays, Anxiety, and Affective Symptomatology among Institutionally Reared Romanian Children." *Journal of the American Academy of Child and Adolescent Psychiatry* 43, no. 10 (2004): 1283-92.

Emmer, Edmund T., Carolyn M. Evertson, and Murray E. Worsham. *Classroom Management for Secondary Teachers (6th ed.).* Boston: Allyn and Bacon, 2002.

Evanski, Gerard. *Classroom Activators (2nd ed.).* Thousand Oaks, CA: Corwin Press, 2008.

Faber, Jean E., John D. Morris, and Mary G. Lieberman. "The Effect of Note Taking on Ninth Grade Students' Comprehension." *Reading Psychology* 21, no. 3 (2000): 257-70.

Ford, Alisha D., D. Joe Olmi, Ron P. Edwards, and Daniel H. Tingstrom. "The Sequential Introduction of Compliance Training Components with Elementary-Aged Children in General Education Classroom Settings." *School Psychology Quarterly* 16, no. 2 (2001): 142-57.

Foster, Michele. "Using Call-and-Response to Facilitate Language Mastery and Literacy Acquisition among African American Students." *ERIC Digest* (July 2002): ERIC Number: ED468194

Francis, Darlene D., Frances A. Champagne, Dong Liu, and Michael J. Meaney. "Maternal Care, Gene Expression, and the Development of Individual Differences in Stress Reactivity." *Annals of the New York Academy of Sciences,* 896 (1999): 66–84.

Fry, R., and G. F. Smith. "The Effects of Feedback and Eye Contact on Performance of a Digit-Coding Task." *Journal of Social Psychology* 96, (1975): 145-46.

Gardner, Ralph, William L. Heward, and Teresa A. Grossi. "Effects of Response Cards on Student Participation and Academic Achievement: A Systematic Replication with Inner-City Students During Whole-Class Science Instruction." *Journal of Applied Behavior Analysis* 27, no. 1 (1994): 63-71.

Gerhard, M. E. "Effects of Headlines and Recaps on Radio News Learning." *Journal of Radio Studies* 1, no.1-2 (1992): 37-42.

Gettinger, Maribeth, and Jill K. Seibert. "Best Practices in Increasing Academic Learning Time." *Best Practices in School Psychology IV* 1 (2002): 773-87.

Goddard, Roger D., Wayne K. Hoy, and Anita Woolfolk Hoy. "Collective Teacher Efficacy: Its Meaning, Measure, and Impact on Student Achievement." *American Educational Research Journal* 37, no. 2 (2000): 479-507.

Goldin-Meadow, S. "How Gesture Promotes Learning Throughout Childhood." *Child Development Perspectives* 1, no. 3 (2009): 106-11.

Goldin-Meadow, S., H. Nusbaum, S. Kelly, and S. Wagner. "Explaining Math: Gesturing Lightens the Load." *Psychological Science* 12, no. 6 (2001): 516-22.

Gorham, Joan. "The Relationship between Verbal Teacher Immediacy Behaviors and Student Learning." *Communication Education* 37, no. 1 (1988): 40-53.

Gorham, J. and D. M. Christophel. "The Relationship of Teachers' Use of Humor in the Classroom to Immediacy and Student Learning." *Communication Education* 39, no. 1, (1990): 46-62.

Grady, Denise. "The Vision Thing: Mainly in the Brain." *Discover* 14, no. 6 (1993): 56-66.

Griffiths, Roger. "Speech Rate and NNS Comprehension: A Preliminary Study in Time-Benefit Analysis." *Language Learning* 40, no. 3 (1990): 311-36.

Gueguen N, and C. Jacob. "Direct Look Versus Evasive Glance and Compliance with a Request." *Journal of Social Psychology* 142, no. 3: (2002): 393-96.

Gueguen, N., and J. Fischer-Lokou. "Hitchhikers' Smiles and Receipt of Help." *Psychological Reports* 94 (2004): 756-60.

Gunter, B. "Recall of Brief Television News Items: Effects of Presentation Mode, Picture Content and Serial Position." *Journal of Educational Television* 5, no. 2 (1979): 57-61.

Hamlet, Carolynn C., Saul Axelrod, and Steven Kuerschner. "Eye Contact as an Antecedent to Compliant Behavior." *Journal of Applied Behavioral Analysis* 17, no. 4 (1984): 553–57.

Heath, Dan, and Chip Heath. "Analysis of Paralysis." *Fast Company* 120 (2007).

Heath, Chip and Dan Heath. *Switch: How to Change Things When Change Is Hard.* New York: Broadway Books, 2010.

Herrnstein, R.J. "Relative and Absolute Strength of Responses as a Function of Frequency of Reinforcement." *Journal of the Experimental Analysis of Behavior* 4, no. 3 (1961): 267–72.

Hollowood, T. M., C. L. Salisbury, B. Rainforth, and M. M. Palombaro. "Use of Instructional Time in Classrooms Serving Students with and without Severe Disabilities." *Exceptional Student*, 61: (1995), 242-53.

Hooper, S., and M. J. Hannafin. "Cooperative CBI: The Effects of Heterogeneous Versus Homogeneous Grouping on the Learning of Progressively Complex Concepts." *Journal of Educational Computing Research* 4, no. 4 (1988): 413-24.

Huelser, B. J., and J. Metcalfe. "Making Related Errors Facilitates Learning, but Learners Do Not Know It." *Memory and Cognition* 40, no. 4 (2012): 514-27.

Hunkin, N. M., A. R. Mayes, L. J. Gregory, A. K. Nicholas, J. A. Nunn, M. J. Brammer, E. T. Bullmore, and S. C. R. Williams. "Novelty-Related Activation within the Medial Temporal Lobes." *Neuropsychologia* 40, no. 8 (2002): 1456-64.

Huot, R. L., K. V. Thrivikraman, M. J. Meaney, and P. M. Plotsky. "Development of Adult Ethanol Preference and Anxiety as a Consequence of Neonatal Maternal Separation in Long Evans Rats and Reversal with Antidepressant Treatment." *Psychopharmacology* 158, no. 4 (2001): 366–73.

Jang, Hyungshim, Johnmarshall Reeve, and Edward L. Deci. "Engaging Students in Learning Activities: It Is Not Autonomy Support or Structure but Autonomy Support and Structure." *Journal of Educational Psychology* 102, no. 3 (2010): 588.

Jiang, Yuhong, Joo-Hyun Song, and Amanda Rigas. "High-Capacity Spatial Contextual Memory." *Psychonomic Bulletin & Review* 12, no. 3 (2005): 524-29.

Kastner, Sabine, Peter De Weerd, Robert Desimone, and Leslie G. Ungerleider. "Mechanisms of Directed Attention in the Human Extrastriate Cortex as Revealed by Functional MRI." Science 282, no. 5386 (1998): 108-11.

Kelley, D. H., and J. Gotham. "Effects of Immediacy on Recall of Information." *Communication Education* 37, no. 3 (1988): 198-207.

Kellam, Sheppard G., George W. Rebok, Nicholas Ialongo, and Lawrence S. Mayer. "The Course and Malleability of Aggressive Behavior from Early First Grade into Middle School: Results of a Developmental Epidemiologically-Based Preventive Trial." *Journal of Child Psychology and Psychiatry* 35, no. 2 (1994): 259-81.

King, Stanley O., and Cedric L. Williams. "Novelty-Induced Arousal Enhances Memory for Cued Classical Fear Conditioning: Interactions between Peripheral Adrenergic and Brainstem Glutamatergic Systems." *Learning & Memory* 16, no. 10 (2009): 625-34.

Kinomura, S., J. Larsson, B. Gulyas, and P. E. Roland. "Activation by Attention of the Human Reticular Formation and Thalamic Intralaminar Nuclei." *Science* 271, no. 5248 (1996): 512–15.

Kirk, K. I., D. B. Pisoni, and R. C. Miyamoto. "Effects of Stimulus Variability on Speech Perception in Listeners with Hearing Impairment." *Journal of Speech, Language, and Hearing Research* 40, no. 6 (1997): 1395-1405.

Kirschner, P. A., J. Sweller, and R. E. Clark. "Why Minimal Guidance during Instruction Does Not Work: An Analysis of the Failure of Constructivist, Discovery, Problem-Based, Experiential, and Inquiry-Based Teaching." *Educational Psychologist* 41, no. 2 (2006): 75-86.

Kleinke, Chris L. "Gaze and Eye Contact: A Research Review." *Psychological Bulletin* 100, no. 1 (1986): 78-100.

Kruglanski, A. W., A. Pierro, L. Mannetti, and E. De Grada. "Groups as Epistemic Providers: Need for Closure and the Unfolding of Group-Centrism." *Psychological review* 113, no. 1 (2006): 84-100.

Lay, Clarry H., and Allan Paivio. "The Effects of Task Difficulty and Anxiety on Hesitations in Speech." *Canadian Journal of Behavioural Science/Revue Canadienne des Sciences du Comportement* 1, no. 1 (1969): 25-37.

Ledoux, Joseph. *The Emotional Brain: The Mysterious Underpinnings of Emotional Life.* New York: Touchstone, 1996.

Leinhardt, Gaea, and James G. Greeno. "The Cognitive Skill of Teaching." *Journal of Educational Psychology* 78, no. 2 (1986): 75-95.

Lesiuk, Teresa. "The Effect of Music Listening on Work Performance." *Psychology of Music* 33, no. 2 (2005): 173-91.

Lewis, James W., Michael S. Beauchamp, and Edgar A. DeYoe. "A Comparison of Visual and Auditory Motion Processing in Human Cerebral Cortex." *Cerebral Cortex* 10, No. 9, (2000): 873-88.

Lubow, R. E., B. Rifkin, and M. Alek. "The Context Effect: The Relationship between Stimulus Preexposure and Environmental Preexposure Determines Subsequent Learning." *Journal of Experimental Psychology: Animal Behavior Processes* 2, no. 1 (1976): 38-47.

Mahl, George F. "Everyday Disturbances of Speech." In *Language in Psychotherapy,* edited by Robert L. Russell, 213-69. Springer: US, 1987.

Martinussen, Rhonda, and Rosemary Tannock. "Working Memory Impairments in Children with Attention-Deficit Hyperactivity Disorder with and without Comorbid Language Learning Disorders." *Journal of Clinical and Experimental Neuropsychology* 28, no. 7 (2006): 1073-94.

Mayer, G. R., and B. Sulzer-Azaroff. "Interventions for Vandalism and Aggression." *Interventions for Academic and Behavior Problems II: Preventive and Remedial Approaches* (2002): 853-84.

McComas, J., A. Thompson, and L. Johnson. "The Effects of Presession Attention on Problem Behavior Maintained by Different Reinforcers." *Journal of Applied Behavior Analysis* 36 (2003): 297–307.

Mehrabian, A., and S. Ferris. "Inference of Attitudes from Nonverbal Communication in Two Channels." *Journal of Consulting Psychology* 31, no. 3 (1967): 248-52.

Menzel, K. E., and L. J. Carrell. "The Impact of Gender and Immediacy on Willingness to Talk and Perceived Learning." *Communication Education* 48, no. 1, (1999): 31-40.

Michon, Pierre-Emmanuel, and Michel Denis. "When and Why Are Visual

Landmarks Used in Giving Directions?" *Lecture Notes in Computer Science* 2205 (2001): 292-305.

Miller, George A. "The Magical Number Seven, Plus or Minus Two: Some Limits on Our Capacity for Processing Information." *Psychological Review* 63, no. 2 (1956): 81–97.

Miller, Norman, Geoffrey Maruyama, Rex J. Beaber, and Keith Valone. "Speed of Speech and Persuasion." *Journal of Personality and Social Psychology* 34, no. 4 (1976): 615-24.

Millis, Barbara J., and Philip G. Cottell, Jr. *Cooperative Learning for Higher Education Faculty.* Phoenix, Arizona: The Oryx Press, 1998.

Mitra, R., S. Jadhav, B. S. McEwen, A. Vyas, and S. Chattarji. "Stress Duration Modulates the Spatiotemporal Patterns of Spine Formation in the Basolateral Amygdala." *Proceedings of the National Academy of Sciences, USA* 102, no. 26 (2005): 9371–76.

Moellenberg, D.R. "Colorado State University Offers Information to Farmers about New Strain of Russian Wheat Aphid Found in Colorado Wheat." *Colorado State University Cooperative Extension News* Release, June 23, 2003.

Morsella, Ezequiel, and Robert M. Krauss. "The Role of Gestures in Spatial Working Memory and Speech." *The American Journal of Psychology* 117 (2004): 411-24.

Narayan, Janani S., William L. Heward, Ralph Gardner, Frances H. Courson, and Christine K. Omness. "Using Response Cards to Increase Student Participation in an Elementary Classroom." *Journal of Applied Behavior Analysis* 23, no. 4 (1990): 483-90.

Ogden, W. R. "Reaching All the Students: The Feedback Lecture." *Journal of Instructional Psychology* 30, no. 1 (2003): 22-27.

Otteson, J. D., and C. R. Otteson. "Effect of Teacher's Gaze on Children's Story Recall." *Perceptual Motor Skill* 50 (1980): 35-42.

Page, Richard A., and Balloun, Joseph L. "The Effect of Voice Volume on the Perception of Personality." *The Journal of Social Psychology* 105, no. 1 (1978): 65-72.

Pashler, H., N. Cepeda, J. T. Wixted, and D. Rohrer. "When Does Feedback Facilitate Learning of Words?" *Journal of Experimental Psychology: Learning, Memory, and Cognition* 31, no. 1 (2005): 3-8.

Pert, Candace B. *Molecules of Emotion: Why You Feel the Way You Feel.* New York: Scribner, 1997.

Pribram, Karl H., and Diane McGuinness. "Arousal, Activation, and Effort in the Control of Attention." *Psychological Review* 82, no. 2 (1975): 116-49.

Preece, Scott Everett. *A Spreading Activation Network Model for Information Retrieval.* University of Illinois at Urbana-Champaign, 1981.

Rao, Sumangala P., and Stephen E. DiCarlo. "Active Learning of Respiratory Physiology Improves Performance on Respiratory Physiology Examinations." *Advances in Physiology Education* 25, no. 2 (2001): 55-61.

Rattan, Aneeta, Catherine Good, and Carol S. Dweck. "It's OK—Not Everyone Can Be Good at Math: Instructors with an Entity Theory Comfort (and Demotivate) Students." *Journal of Experimental Social Psychology* 48, no. 3 (2012): 731-37.

Ross, John A. "Teacher Efficacy and the Effects of Coaching on Student Achievement." *Canadian Journal of Education/Revue Canadienne de L'education* 17, no. 1 (1992): 51-65.

Rayneri, Letty J., Brian L. Gerber, and Larry P. Wiley. "Gifted Achievers and Gifted Underachievers: The Impact of Learning Style Preferences in the Classroom." *Prufrock Journal* 14, no. 4 (2003): 197-204.

Rowe, Mary Budd. "Wait Time and Rewards as Instructional Variables, Their Influence in Language, Logic and Fate Control. *Paper presented at the National Association for Research in Science Teaching,* Chicago, Ill., 1972.

Rowe, Mary Budd. "Wait Time: Slowing Down May Be a Way of Speeding Up!" *Journal of Teacher Education* 37, no. 1 (1986): 43-50.

Rule, Audrey C., C. Jolene Dockstader, and Roger A. Stewart. "Hands-On and Kinesthetic Activities for Teaching Phonological Awareness." *Early Childhood Education Journal* 34, no. 3 (2006):195-201.

Salimpoor, V. N., M. Benovoy, K. Larcher, A. Dagher, and R. J. Zatorre. "Anatomically Distinct Dopamine Release During Anticipation and Experience of Peak Emotion to Music." *Nature Neuroscience* 14, no. 2 (2011): 257-62.

Schachter, Stanley, Nicholas Christenfeld, Bernard Ravina, and Frances Bilous. "Speech Disfluency and the Structure of Knowledge." *Journal of Personality and Social Psychology* 60, no. 3 (1991): 362-67.

Scherer, Klaus R., Harvey London, and Jared J. Wolf. "The Voice of Confidence: Paralinguistic Cues and Audience Evaluation." *Journal of Research in Personality* 7, no. 1, (1973): 31-44.

Schleuder, Joan D., Alice V. White, and Glen T. Cameron. "Priming Effects of Television News Bumpers and Teasers on Attention and Memory." *Journal of Broadcasting & Electronic Media* 37, no. 4 (1993): 437-52.

Shamo, G. Wayne, and Linda M. Meador. "The Effect of Visual Distraction upon Recall and Attitude Change." *Journal of Communication* 19, no. 2 (1969): 157-62.

Sherwood, J.V. "Facilitative Effects of Gaze upon Learning." *Perceptual Motor Skill* 64, no. 3 Part 2 (1988): 1275-78.

Shoemaker, Pamela J. "Hardwired for News: Using Biological and Cultural Evolution to Explain the Surveillance Function." *Journal of Communication* 46, no. 3 (1996): 32-47.

Shriberg, Elizabeth. "Spontaneous Speech: How People Really Talk and Why Engineers Should Care." Paper presented at the meeting of the *INTERSPEECH*, 2005.

Singer, Melissa A., and Susan Goldin-Meadow. "Children Learn When Their Teacher's Gestures and Speech Differ." *Psychological Science* 16, no. 2 (2005): 85-9.

Slavin, Robert E. "Ability Grouping in Secondary Schools: A Response to Hallinan." *Review of Educational Research* (1990): 505-7.

Smith, M. K., W. B. Wood, W. K. Adams, C. Wieman, J. K. Knight, N. Guild, and T. T. Su. "Why Peer Discussion Improves Student Performance on In-Class Concept Questions." *Science* 323, no. 5910 (2009): 122-24.

Smith, Steven M. "Background Music and Context-Dependent Memory." *The American Journal of Psychology* 98 (1985): 591-603.

Snyder, J. "Reinforcement and Coercion Mechanism in the Development of Antisocial Behavior: Peer Relationships." *Antisocial Behavior in Children and Adolescents: A Developmental Analysis and Model for Intervention* (2002): 101-22.

Son, Jinak, Stephen D. Reese, and William R. Davie. "Effects of Visual-Verbal Redundancy and Recaps on Television News Learning." *Journal of Broadcasting & Electronic Media* 31, no. 2 (1987): 207-16.

Sparrow, B., J. Liu, and D. M. Wegner. "Google Effects on Memory: Cognitive Consequences of Having Information at Our Fingertips." *Science* 333, no. 6043 (2011): 776-78.

Stahl, Robert J. "Using Think-Time and Wait-Time Skillfully in the Classroom."

ERIC Digest (May 1994): ERIC Number: ED370885.

Stahl, Robert J. *Using "Think-Time" Behaviors to Promote Students' Information Processing, Learning, and On-Task Participation: An Instructional Module.* Tempe, AZ: Arisona State University, 1990.

Steriade, M. "Arousal: Revisiting the Reticular Activating System." *Science* 272, no. 5259 (1996): 225–26.

Sutherland, K. S., and J. H. Wehby. "Exploring the Relationship Between Increased Opportunities to Respond to Academic Requests and the Academic and Behavioral Outcomes of Students with EBD: A Review." *Remedial and Special Education* 22, no. 2 (2001): 113-21.

Sutoo, Den'etsu, and Kayo Akiyama. "Music Improves Dopaminergic Neurotransmission: Demonstration Based on the Effect of Music on Blood Pressure Regulation." *Brain Research* 1016, no. 2 (2004): 255-62.

Theeuwes, Jan. "Cross-Dimensional Perceptual Selectivity." *Perception & Psychophysics* 50, no. 2 (1991): 184-93.

Thorndike, Edward L. *The Psychology of Learning.* New York: Teachers College, 1914.

Tuckman, Bruce W., and Thomas L. Sexton. "The Effect of Teacher Encouragement on Student Self-Efficacy and Motivation for Self-Regulated Performance." *Journal of Social Behavior & Personality* (1991).

U.S. Department of Education. "The Final Report of the National Mathematics Advisory Council." Washington, D.C.: Education Publications Center, U.S. Department of Education (2008).

Valenzeno, L., M. Alibali, and R. Klatzky. "Teachers' Gestures Facilitate Students' Learning: A Lesson in Symmetry." *Contemporary Educational Psychology* 28, no. 2, (2003): 187–204.

Vallecorsa, Ada, Laurie Ungerleider DeBettencourt, Naomi Zigmond, and Ann Castel Davis. *Students with Mild Disabilities in General Education Settings: A Guide for Special Educators.* New York: Prentice Hall, 1999.

Van Ijzendoorn, M. H., and F. Juffer. "The Emanuel Miller Memorial Lecture 2006: Adoption as Intervention: Meta-Analytic Evidence for Massive Catch-Up and Plasticity in Physical, Socio-emotional, and Cognitive Development." *Journal of Child Psychology and Psychiatry* 47, no. 12 (2006): 1228-45.

Ververs, Patricia May, and Christopher D. Wickens. "Head-Up Displays: Effect of Clutter, Display Intensity, and Display Location on Pilot Performance." *The*

International Journal of Aviation Psychology 8, no. 4 (1998): 377-403.

White, L., N. Spada, P. M. Lightbown, and L. Ranta. "Input Enhancement and L2 Question Formation." *Applied Linguistics* 12, no. 4 (1991): 416-32.

Wilen, William W., Ed. *Questions, Questioning Techniques, and Effective Teaching.* Washington, DC: National Education Association (1987).

Williams, J. R. "Guidelines for the Use of Multimedia in Instruction." *Proceedings of the Human Factors and Ergonomics Society 42nd Annual Meeting* (1998): 1447-51.

Wu, Ying Choon, and Seanna Coulson. "How Iconic Gestures Enhance Communication: An ERP Study." *Brain and Language* 101, no. 3 (2006): 234-45.

Yamagata, T., Y. Nakayama, J. Tanji, and E. Hoshi. "Distinct Information Representation and Processing for Goal-Directed Behavior in the Dorsolateral and Ventrolateral Prefrontal Cortex and the Dorsal Premotor Cortex." *Journal of Neuroscience* 32, no. 37 (2012): 12934-49.

Yarbrough, C., and H. Price. "Prediction of Performer Attentiveness Based on Rehearsal Activity and Teacher Behavior." *Journal of Research in Music Education* 29, no. 3 (1981): 209-217.

Zhao, Y. "The Effects of Listeners' Control of Speech Rate on Second Language Comprehension." *Applied Linguistics* 18, no. 1 (1997): 49-68.

CPSIA information can be obtained at www.ICGtesting.com
Printed in the USA
LVOW09s1450200416

484522LV00011B/262/P